"An indispensable guide for clinicians se
into emotional management. Erica uses her expertise to distil art
therapy's principles and turn anger management into an enjoyable,
impactful journey for both practitioners and clients."

—Nadia Paredes, LMFT, ATR

"Erica Curtis is a master at taking complicated emotions like anger, a
feeling that seems so intimidating and overwhelming to most of us,
and providing expertly organized and practical strategies that anyone will benefit from using. She provides 70 creative and inventive
exercises that will get you thinking about anger from a much more
compassionate perspective. I look forward to using Erica's art therapy
exercises in my sessions with clients in the future!"

—Risa Williams, therapist and award-winning author of
*The Ultimate Time Management Toolkit, The Ultimate
Anxiety Toolkit* and *The Ultimate Self-Esteem Toolkit*

"With creativity, a wealth of knowledge, expertise, and skill, Erica
Curtis delivers a masterful step-by-step book for mental health pro-
viders to put therapeutic art activities into practice immediately. This
is a much-needed guide to acknowledge, access, and express anger
through the healing application of expressive art."

—Marci Dadd, clinical art therapist, LMFT

"An ingeniously constructive way to explore the relationship with
anger. Thoughtful guidelines to promote healing and decrease harm for
trained clinicians experimenting with creativity in therapeutic practice for the first time. A straightforward, adaptive, and user-friendly
resource most useful for art therapists or art therapist trainees."

—Louvenia Jackson, Ph.D., LMFT, ATR-BC, author of *Cultural
Humility in Art Therapy*, associate professor and Department
Chair of the Marital and Family Therapy with Specialization
in Art Therapy Department at Loyola Marymount University

Introduction

Anger can be loud, intimidating, or aggressive. It can also be timid, motivating, or kind. How anger is expressed or suppressed determines how helpful or harmful it is. Anger isn't bad. It empowers, encourages change, and helps resolve past hurts. However, because of anger's volatile potential, working with anger takes a delicate balance of expression and restraint. Creativity is a key ingredient to navigating this balance. And we need creative approaches to working with anger more than ever.

More people feel angrier, more intensely, more often than ever (see, for example, Fleming 2022; Gallup 2022; World Economic Forum 2019). Even before the 2020 Covid-19 pandemic's social, emotional, and economic impact, research revealed current generations were angrier than a generation ago (Hensley 2019). Whatever age, treatment unit, or sub-specialty you work with, the likelihood of encountering anger has dramatically increased, even if it is not your specialty. When anger does not spontaneously appear, I hope that this book will give you the confidence and curiosity to creatively awaken it.

This book will guide you to access creativity's unique change-making properties when working with anger. You will learn arts-based activities to cultivate emotional flexibility and decrease destructive patterns as well as activate and direct anger for positive transformation. As a seasoned mental health professional, writer, and speaker, I am intrigued by what creates change. I have spent decades synthesizing what I observe to be the most effective approaches to wellbeing. In addition to neurobiology, trauma research, mindfulness, cognitive-behavioral practices, and positive psychology, I maintain deep roots in art therapy. Research on art-making's inherent therapeutic value is ever expanding, and after more than 20 years working as a board-certified art therapist, my awe at art's transformative properties endures. It is not an exaggeration to say that I see change happen every day. I hope you will, too.

How to use this book

This book offers mental health professionals step-by-step art activities to skillfully work with anger's varied forms, including explosive anger that requires soothing, repressed anger that needs releasing, and justice-induced anger that craves direction. While the activities are engaging, they are more than simply entertaining ways to revisit a challenging issue. All the activities within this book are based on art therapy theory and practice. As such, I have thoughtfully selected art materials and carefully crafted instructions, processes, and reflection questions to target specific therapeutic goals related to anger.

The book is divided into two parts. Part I contains everything you need to know to get started, including a framework of how art creates change, and why it is uniquely suited to working with anger. In this part you will also learn the fundamentals for responding to the art-making process and art product. Because no experience with art or art therapy is necessary to use this book, this part concludes with helpful tips for comfortably working within your scope of training and expertise.

Part II offers 70 therapeutic art activities divided equally among seven chapters. Each activity addresses a different therapeutic goal: Self-Care, Get to Know Anger, Recruit Other Emotions, Soothe Anger, Awaken Anger, Harness Anger, and Navigate Anger in Relationships. Chapters do not need to be worked through in sequence, and neither do the activities within the chapters. However, the order of chapters emphasizes the therapeutic importance of establishing certain skills before attempting others. For example, clients need emotional regulation skills through self-care practices before getting to know, awakening, or harnessing anger.

Each of the 70 activities includes a brief explanation of its relevance to the chapter theme, and how it will create meaningful change. Materials, step-by-step instructions, and discussion questions are also included. Helpful tips describe adaptations for diverse needs such as age and developmental considerations, comfort level with self-expression, and common challenges—after all, effective therapy does not use a cookie-cutter approach. Adjust the activities as needed to fit individual client or group needs.

All 70 activities as marked with a ★ can be downloaded from https://library.jkp.com/redeem using the code DYPJFCQ

Getting started

This book is designed to flexibly meet your clients' needs as they learn to safely feel, express, and benefit from anger.

Create space. Prepare a flat surface for materials and art-making. If space is sparse, be resourceful. A TV tray, clipboard, or floor may suffice. Consider space for securely and confidentially storing client art if you will be holding on to it for safe keeping or referring to it another time. For example, store art in clients' files or fold large sheets of construction paper in half to use as art folders. Secure these in a drawer or file cabinet.

Gather materials. Most activities require readily available, inexpensive materials such as printer paper and common coloring materials like colored pens, pencils, markers, or crayons. Keep these accessible. If art supplies are unavailable, office supplies like a pen and sticky notes will suffice for many activities. A small number of activities require other materials like collage images from magazines or printouts from online, scissors, a glue stick, tape or a stapler, colored construction paper, a ruler, colored pipe cleaners, a black marker, or a note card or blank postcard.

Commit to creativity. It is easy to default to traditional talk strategies if art-making is foreign to you, if you have strayed away from it, or if you're introducing art-making to someone new. Increase your confidence-facilitating therapeutic art activities by first trying the activities yourself outside of sessions. When with a client, share that you have been learning creative approaches and explain art-making's therapeutic benefits (found in Part I, "What Is Art Therapy?"). Ask if they would be interested in trying something new.

Make time. Activities will take between 10 and 20 minutes, including discussion time. Clients may take more or less time on a given activity, and discussion time will vary depending on questions and client engagement. Consider introducing an art activity within the first half of your session, to allow plenty of time for activity completion and discussion. If a client hasn't finished the activity, or discussion time needs to be cut short, simply let them know you will pick up where you left off next time.

Select an activity. You do not need to familiarize yourself with all the activities before starting. Peruse a chapter that is most applicable to a current therapeutic stage or goal, and begin there. As you become more familiar with the activities, you will be able to select the activities spontaneously to capitalize on crucial therapeutic moments. Use one or more activities in a session. Repeat activities that are particularly helpful. Consider providing clients with copies of self-care and soothing activities for home use.

Part I

FUNDAMENTALS OF WORKING WITH ANGER CREATIVELY

WHAT IS ART THERAPY?

Art therapy uses tailored art-making experiences to address specific emotional, relational, and mental health needs. This is accomplished by integrating knowledge of art-making's unique therapeutic properties with human development and psychology. Art therapy involves thoughtful consideration of sensory experience, imagination, activity instructions, process and product, and reflection questions. While only credentialed art therapists, or those working toward credentialing, can facilitate art therapy, other mental health professionals, educators, and even caregivers can guide art therapy-inspired activities with valuable results.

How art therapy works is multifaceted. For convenience and simplicity, I created the acronym, ARTS, to explain its fundamental principles. ARTS stands for: Access, Reflection, Transformation, and Social:

Access: Creative expression gives access to thoughts and feelings even when verbal communication is limited due to age, development, trauma, or heightened stress. Art's sensory qualities also help clients to access and communicate complex nuances of emotions through color, size, texture, and form.

Reflection: Clients gain distance from thoughts, feelings, and experiences by reflecting on their art products. Separation decreases emotional overwhelm, re-engages the thinking mind, and sparks new insights. What's more, reflecting on the art-making process trains here-and-now attention to internal experiences, and highlights ways clients may approach or respond to other tasks in real life.

Transformation: Transformation takes place on multiple levels. Different art materials stimulate varied internal responses. Creative imagination promotes cognitive and emotional flexibility (see, for example, Roberts *et al.* 2017; Veraksa, Gavrilova, and Veraksa 2022). Moreover, clients can transform how they relate to thoughts, feelings, and memories by literally transforming their art through adding, redacting, scrunching, and folding, as well as other forms of material manipulation.

Social: Art-making happens within a caring, non-judgmental therapeutic relationship where the therapist models and encourages curiosity. At times, relationship-focused art activities are used to strengthen connections or practice healthy boundaries within families or communities, or between the client and therapist.

I invite you to use the acronym ARTS to easily explain the therapeutic benefits of art therapy-inspired activities to your clients and your colleagues.

HOW ART THERAPY HELPS ANGER

Anger intends to protect us, but easily causes unnecessary hurt. Whether prompted by a past, present, or imagined unfairness, boundary violation, or vulnerability, anger turns up nervous system activation. Heart rate, breath, and muscle tension increase to fight or avoid threats. Problem solving, logic, and effective communication are impaired. If an agitated state persists, or if anger spikes quickly, the nervous system may prompt aggression or shift into collapse, resulting in disconnection, lethargy, or hopelessness. Neither option is optimal, and rarely does either bring resolution. A healthy relationship with anger requires finding a sweet spot where anger can be felt and expressed without overwhelming oneself or others.

Art-making provides an emotional outlet that is simultaneously expressive as well as containing. The creative process itself permits release of emotional energy as well as a safe avenue to communicate ideas and feelings. Meanwhile, carefully chosen art materials and instructions inform the limits of expression. For example, a large piece of paper invites big movements and offers ample space for feelings and ideas to flow. A small piece of paper requires small gestures and editing ideas. Some clients welcome more expressivity while others require more limits. Helping clients find their own creative sweet spot between expression and restraint helps anger-averse clients safely connect with and express this uncomfortable emotion, while giving quick-to-anger clients practice reining it in.

Art therapy also helps clients build a healthy relationship with anger through its emphasis on personal imagery rather than popular metaphors, such as monsters or volcanoes. Encouraging clients to develop their own anger-inspired imagery rapidly leads to new insights about the meaning, role, and origin of anger in their own life. Furthermore, the process of separating anger from oneself by creating personal imagery replicates the process of observing anger with distance and curiosity when it arises in daily life. Ultimately, the practice of acknowledging, separating from, and observing emotion accelerates clients' ability to respond, rather than react, to anger.

WHAT THE SCIENCE SAYS

Human nervous systems function optimally when cues of emotional, relational, and physical safety are present (Porges 2022). In a mobilized state, such as anger, the body shifts away from maintenance, growth, and repair functions toward functions of immediate survival. Once the threat is alleviated, the nervous system returns to its biological home of stability. However, adverse life events, trauma, and chronic stress force the nervous system to develop what author Deb Dana calls a biological "home away from home" (Sunseri 2019). The nervous system shifts more rapidly into a mobilized or immobilized state, it remains there longer, and more situations are misperceived as threatening. In many cases, the nervous system not only needs cues of safety to return to healthy functioning; it also needs to relearn that it is safe to feel safe.

Research supports that art experiences have unique properties that guide the nervous system back to its natural state of wellbeing. Biomarkers of stress drop following free choice art-making (Kaimal, Kendra, and Muniz 2016)—a UK medical program examining arts interventions showed a 20 percent reduction in healthcare interventions following arts experiences (Fancourt and Finn 2019). What is more, arts-based tasks have been shown to outperform non-artistic stress-reducing tasks in lowering stress (Abbott, Shanahan, and Neufeld 2013). Whether we're harnessing art-making's unique sensory and kinesthetic properties (see, for example, Lusebrink 2014; Nan, Hinz, and Lusebrink 2021), accessing its ability to focus the mind on the present moment (see Hinchey 2018; Newland and Bettencourt 2020), using it to connect individuals to their internal and external resources (see Martin *et al.* 2018), or exploiting the ability of art to consolidate memories (see Hass-Cohen and Clyde Findlay 2019) and shift perspectives (see, for example, Segal-Engelchin *et al.* 2020; Segal-Engelchin, Huss, and Sarid 2021), simply stated, art-making makes us healthier.

THE ESSENTIALS

Adopt a creative framework

I think of working with anger creatively like conducting an orchestra, in which each instrument represents an emotion. Anger has a role and a purpose, just like a strings, wind, or percussion section. Rather than silencing anger, a creative conductor uses anger in nuanced ways to enrich the overall song. At key points, the conductor encourages anger to come to the forefront. At other times, the conductor guides anger to quiet down so other emotions are heard, or to bring about resolution. As you select activities, consider using this creative framework, along with your clinical skills, to decide when to safely amplify, hush, or harmonize anger.

Educate clients about therapeutic art-making

Explain that art-making helps us think and communicate about anger in very important ways that differ from talking alone. Emphasize that aesthetics and artistic skill are unimportant. This is not an art class. Share how art therapy works, referring to the earlier section "What Is Art Therapy?"

Reassure teen and adult clients that people commonly stop making art after childhood, and that it is fine to approach activities in any manner. If a client remarks that they do not know what to create, reassure them that it is okay not to know. I often tell clients, "Creativity comes from a not-knowing place," and I encourage them to share ideas they would otherwise dismiss because they seem nonsensical or unrelated.

Meet clients where they are

As a professional, you know how to meet clients where they are by individualizing and cocreating care with them. Keep the following additional tips in mind to bridge your own expectations when using art activities with client responses and needs:

- Some activities in this book offer metaphors as a creative starting point or to help with psychoeducation. Ask your clients if the metaphors are relatable or if another metaphor comes to mind that they would prefer.

- For simplicity, activities regularly refer to "anger" in descriptions, instructions, and discussion questions. Replace the word "anger" with whatever variation of this emotion is most suitable to your client, such as "irritated," "annoyed," or "upset." If a client insists that they do not feel anger, focus activities on whatever feeling they describe, including "bored," "tired," "indifferent," or "nothing." Use clients' own words whenever possible.

- Proactively give permission to disagree and decline. When offering instructions, dialogue questions, or observations, include the phrase "or not." For example, "Would you like to give this a title, or not?" and "Did you notice any changes inside, or not?"

- Adapt language in the activities and discussion questions to meet your client's age and developmental level.

- It is okay to shorten, pause, or shift from one activity to another as needed.

Maximize the art-making process

The art-making process is as therapeutically valuable as the resulting image. While discussion questions that follow the activities in Part II will guide process-focused reflections, here are some helpful fundamentals to keep in mind:

- Every person has the potential to respond to the same stimulus differently. Activities designed to calm or excite emotion may have the opposite effect. This does not mean that the activity has failed. Regardless of whether your client finds an art activity pleasant, unpleasant, or neutral, their thoughts and feelings offer an insight into their internal world and patterns that arise elsewhere in their life.

- The art-making process can stimulate frustration ("I messed up"), anxiety ("I'm probably doing this wrong"), and self-criticism ("I'm horrible at this"). Use your clinical judgment to decide whether to reassure your clients or teach them the value of reassuring themselves. This is an opportunity to prompt your client to practice any number of strategies for dealing with unwanted or unhelpful thoughts. If you are unfamiliar with strategies for dealing with unwanted or unhelpful thoughts, consider using the suggestion in the next bullet point.

- Art-making has a present-focused quality we can intentionally tap into. If a client's mind gets stuck in self-judgment or overwhelm, invite them to focus on a single pleasant sensory experience related to the art-making process, such as the color they are using or a repetitive motion they are making. Remind your client to notice when their mind wanders, and to return it to their chosen focus point.

- Art-making requires problem solving. Share strength-based observations and invite clients to reflect on strategies they used. Did your client dive right in or take their time? Did they work with mistakes or start over? Were they spontaneous or methodical? Explore how their approach helped with the art activity and where a similar strategy could serve them in daily life.

Maximize talking about art

Talking or writing about personal art is not always necessary to achieve therapeutic goals. However, helping clients put words to images can offer additional benefits including stimulating new insights, strengthening critical thinking skills (Bowen, Greene, and Kisida 2014), and supporting emotional regulation through naming emotions (Lieberman *et al.* 2007; Torre and Lieberman 2018). Use the discussion questions following the activity instructions in Part II to initiate conversation and deepen clients' meaningful reflections. But first, review these general guidelines to maximize the therapeutic benefits of talking about client art:

- Refrain from evaluative comments such as "Nice work" or "This looks good." Well-meaning remarks like these emphasize artistic merit, which undermines the focus on personal meaning.

- Begin a dialogue with, "Tell me about what you made" or "Let's talk about what's going on in your image." Do not say what you think it is, even if you are certain that you know. Let clients assign their own meaning to their images.

- Make objective observations to deepen client reflections. Start with "I see" or "I notice" followed by an observation of what you literally see. For example, "I see many different shapes over here. Tell me about that."

- Model curiosity to deepen your client's state of curiosity and self-reflection. Begin questions with "I wonder..." For example, "I wonder if blue has special meaning for you, or not?"

- Uncovering and discussing art's personal meaning requires multiple interpersonal, emotional, and cognitive skills. If clients struggle to respond to open-ended questions, provide simpler or more structured options. For example, ask your client to give the image a title, or invite them to describe it in just one, two, or three words.

Work within your scope

In this part you have learned how art-making produces powerful therapeutic change. In Part II you will learn therapeutic art activities informed by art therapy. Whenever learning new approaches, it is important to take precautions, so benefits are maximized and risks minimized. Here are some helpful considerations:

- The art activities in this book were designed with a high degree of containment in mind to minimize sensory over-stimulation, frustration, and emotional overwhelm. This includes limiting activities to structured art materials, such as pencils, markers, collage images, and pipe cleaners. Detailed step-by-step instructions also provide a higher level of containment. Use the recommended materials and instructions unless you are trained in the therapeutic use of variations in art materials and interventions, and you are aware of their contraindications.

- If you are new to working with art or with anger, or if you have aggressive clients, stick with resource-boosting activities that build coping skills, resilience, positive self-talk, and problem-solving skills. You will find activities like these primarily in the following chapters: Self-Care (1), Get to Know Anger (2), Recruit Other Emotions (3), and Soothe Anger (4).

- Use your clinical judgment to assess the appropriateness of any activity before using it, especially when using activities designed to elicit, actively use, or connect deeply with anger. Such activities are primarily found in the following chapters: Awaken Anger (5), Harness Anger (6), and Navigate Anger in Relationships (7).

- Avoid sharp materials when working with clients at risk for violence. Markers may be more suitable than sharp pencils. Suggest tearing magazine pictures instead of offering scissors.

- Describe your experience accurately. If creative tools are new to you, let clients know you are trying a new approach. If you are not an art therapist, explain that you are using art-based interventions, and not art therapy. To practice art therapy requires specialized graduate education, postgraduate supervision by a credentialed art therapist, and oversight by the Art Therapy Credentials Board.

KEY TAKEAWAYS

In this part, we have examined how art therapy works and why it is uniquely suited to working with anger. We have also outlined some essential tips for using art in therapy. Here are some key takeaways:

- Credentialed art therapists facilitate art therapy. However, other mental health professionals, educators, and caregivers can also guide art therapy-inspired activities with valuable results.

- How art therapy works is conveniently captured by the acronym ARTS, which stands for Access, Reflection, Transformation, and Social.

- Art-making helps clients experience anger without overwhelm by providing an emotional outlet that is inherently containing.

- Rather than relying on popular metaphors such as monsters or volcanoes, therapeutic art-making encourages clients to develop personal imagery, which leads to rapid new insights about the meaning, role, and origin of anger in their own life.

- Research supports that art experiences have unique properties that guide the nervous system back to its natural state of wellbeing.

Part II

70 ART THERAPY-INSPIRED ACTIVITIES

Chapter 1

SELF-CARE

Self-care is more than leisure time. Enjoyable, restful, and pleasant activities train the mind and body to feel safe, calm, and connected. This builds resilience, improving our long-term ability to express and rebound from anger more easily (Azarnioshan *et al.* 2019; Doyle, Campbell, and Gryshchuk 2021; Tselebis *et al.* 2022). Therefore, self-care activities can be used to decrease reactivity in the moment *and* to lay the foundation for enduring emotional flexibility. The more we experience states of calm, the more accessible problem-solving and communication skills are, even when we become agitated. This builds momentum toward healthier ways of being in relationship with oneself and with others.

This chapter contains 10 creative activities to bolster self-care for clients and professionals alike. You will find activities that introduce new forms of self-care, challenge barriers to self-care, and amplify self-care benefits. Use the activities in this chapter early and often. Like assembling a first-aid kit, identify which self-care activities are most helpful to your clients so you can quickly employ them when clients show signs of distress or need extra closure at the end of sessions. I also invite you to personally use brief self-care activities to reset before or after sessions—let's not underestimate the importance of taking a quick calming moment for ourselves.

★ SHADES OF "OKAY"

People generally prefer being content to feeling angry. However, when people anger often, being okay may feel foreign or even intolerable. The mind and body may not trust that feeling okay is safe. This can also be true for those who suppress anger. Numbing anger may result in numbing many experiences, including pleasant ones. Feeling relaxed or happy may be too far of a reach. As such, developing self-care practices must include activities that help clients recognize, reconnect with, and tolerate various shades of "okay-ness."

Materials: Drawing paper (any paper works), drawing utensils with a wide range of colors (colored pencils, markers, or crayons)

1. Create a spectrum of "okay" feelings by drawing a long, narrow, horizontal rectangle. Label one end "high-energy okay" and the other "low-energy okay."

2. Give examples of high- and low-energy "okay" feelings. For example, high-energy "okay" feelings could include excited, happy, or playful. Low-energy "okay" feelings could include peaceful, relaxed, or connected.

3. Ask your client to think of a recent time that they felt "okay," even if the feeling was brief or subtle. Ask them to write the feeling along the spectrum based on how low or high energy the experience felt.

4. Invite your client to select a color to represent the feeling. Prompt them to color a small corresponding section of the rectangle.

5. Prompt your client to identify other "okay" feelings they have experienced, to select corresponding colors, and color in the relevant portion of the spectrum, from low to high energy.

6. Provide further creative options, such as coloring lightly for barely felt emotions and darker for strongly felt emotions.

Discussion questions:

- When you look at the completed spectrum, what do you notice? What colors stand out to you?

- Was it easier to recall okay feelings that were high energy, low energy, or somewhere in the middle?

- What types of okay feelings would you like to seek out during the week? Which would be easiest to evoke and savor? How might you do that?

Helpful tip: Providing many different colors increases options for exploring variability in emotions. However, some clients may feel overwhelmed by too many choices. Ask your clients if they enjoy a lot of choice, or if they prefer one of each basic color. Even this simple question is an opportunity for clients to identify a pleasurable preference.

★ PATHS TO SELF-CARE

Self-care is simple, but not easy. It requires prioritizing personal wellbeing while also negotiating others' needs, navigating obstacles, and choosing between conflicting activities, all while weighing up the short- and long-term benefits. No wonder it is difficult to practice self-care. This activity uses creative problem solving to help clients identify a wide range of self-care practices, acknowledge barriers, and circumvent obstacles to establish more effective paths to self-care.

Materials: Drawing paper (any paper works), drawing utensils (colored pencils, markers, or crayons)

1. Explain that your client will make a bubble map. Ask your client to write the word "self-care" in the center of their paper, and to draw a circle around it.

2. Direct your client to write relevant self-care categories around their paper, such as "physical," "mental," "emotional," "social," "financial," and "spiritual."

3. Invite your client to circle the categories and to draw lines connecting the center "self-care" circle to each outer category circle.

4. Direct your client to write down specific self-care acts related to each corresponding category. These should be circled, with connecting lines added to their respective categories.

5. Help your client consider barriers or conflicts preventing self-care. Invite your client to draw barriers using colors, lines, shapes, words, or symbols.

6. Ask, "How can you change your image to make self-care more possible?" Provide options such as adding, removing, or embellishing elements of the drawing. Remind your client that creative solutions can be conceptual or literal.

Discussion questions:

- Does anything stand out when looking at your image? Do you notice any patterns or themes when looking at the self-care practices?

- What feelings arise when you look at the barriers or conflicts in your image?

- Describe how you altered the image to make self-care more accessible. What clues might that give you about handling self-care barriers or conflicts in real life?

Helpful tip: Some clients will benefit from a bubble map's logical style. Others will benefit from a more playful framework. For metaphoric thinkers or young clients, substitute the bubble map for a road or river of self-care. Self-care categories and barriers or obstacles can be represented as cars and potholes on a road or boats and boulders in a river.

★ PLEASING PATTERNS

Our subconscious constantly scans the environment for cues of safety or threat. Sustained, intentional focus on pleasant experiences, whether through taste, touch, sight, smell, or sound, boosts signals of wellbeing. Use this activity to teach clients to savor micro-moments of comfort or pleasure in their everyday surroundings. As they do so, your clients will learn to notice that even mundane calming cues can create significant shifts in their mind and body.

Materials: Drawing paper (any paper works), pencil, drawing utensils (colored pencils, markers, or crayons)

1. Discuss the de-stressing benefits of looking for cues of calm, safety, or comfort in any environment.

2. Invite your client to scan the environment for objects, colors, or textures that evoke curiosity or enjoyment. They may also inspect personal items such as a watch, jewelry, or other belongings.

3. Ask your client to identify one, two, or three pleasing objects to place on top of their paper to trace. They may be objects that represent something comforting. For example, a house key may represent the comfort of home.

4. If the objects are immovable or large, encourage creative problem solving like tracing a small part of the object, producing a texture rubbing, or free hand drawing a simple outline of the object.

5. Suggest your client makes a pattern, tracing the same object or objects multiple times. They may overlap tracings, create a thoughtful composition, or place them randomly.

6. Invite your client to decorate or color the resulting pattern of pleasing objects.

Discussion questions:

- What can you tell me about why you selected these objects?

- What did you notice in your mind and body as you searched for objects? What did you notice as you traced them?

- Did you notice anything unpleasant, bothersome, or distracting during this activity?

Helpful tip: Drawing materials may not be available in everyday stress-inducing situations. Explain that clients can instead trace the outside of pleasant objects with their eyes, or run their finger around the perimeter of a comforting object. Practice this together.

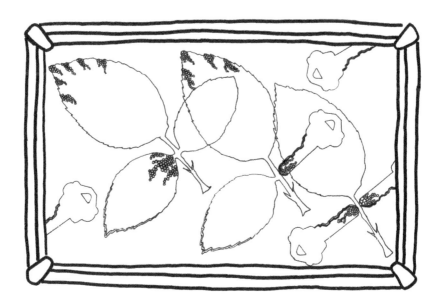

★ POSITIVE TRAIT PRESERVER

Anger can overshadow positive traits such as kindness, persistence, and honesty. Because anger distorts thoughts and prompts behaviors that may not align with someone's core principles, some clients may begin over-identifying with anger, labeling themselves an "angry person." As such, self-care must include preserving and honoring personal strengths as much as it involves taking time to relax or nurture interests. Use this activity to help clients reconnect with their positive traits to help them identify as a whole individual who is so much more than their anger.

Materials: Drawing paper (any paper works), drawing utensils (colored pencils, markers, or crayons)

1. Invite your client to draw basic shapes like diamonds, circles, or squares. Explain that each will represent one of their positive traits or abilities.

2. Optionally, invite your client to think of a metaphor for their positive traits, such as precious gems, lost puzzle pieces, or fragile bubbles.

3. Help your client brainstorm their positive traits by asking, "What do you like about yourself?" "What do others like about you?" "What about you helps you in relationships or work/school settings?"

4. Direct your client to write one positive trait in each shape, adding more shapes as needed. Provide the option to leave shapes empty to represent a characteristic that is yet to be discovered.

5. Ask your client to read each trait, starting with the phrase "I am…" Direct them to pay attention to which statements feel very true, moderately true, and barely true.

6. Invite your client to assign a different color to each of the three categories: very true, moderately true, and barely true. Prompt

them to color each shape with its relevant color, based on how connected they feel to the trait.

Discussion questions:

- Tell me about the shapes and colors you selected. Do they have any particular significance, or not?

- Looking at the whole image, what stands out to you? How do you feel about the positive traits you included?

- What would you need to do, see, hear, or know for your traits to feel even truer about you? Is that in your control, or not?

Helpful tip: Take this activity a step further. Invite your client to embellish one, two, or three traits they value or respect most, regardless of how strongly they feel the trait describes them. Discuss the actions that embody that trait.

★ PRESENT MOMENT PATCHWORK

Meditation is essential hygiene for the mind and body. Meditation can provide quick calming benefits and over time strengthens self-observation, emotional regulation, and non-reactivity, to name just a few (Iani *et al.* 2019; Klussman *et al.* 2020; Wu *et al.* 2019). Yet even with many well-recorded benefits, many resist meditation because for some, it may provoke agitation, anxiety, and restlessness. Meditation is not as easy as it seems, and some clients may quickly decide they are no good at it. This creative activity offers an active alternative to traditional meditation so clients can more comfortably practice non-judgmental awareness of each present moment.

Materials: Sticky notes, drawing or writing utensils, piece of paper (optional)

1. Explain that meditation involves selecting a focal point, noticing when the mind wanders from it, and then returning to the focal point. Common focal points are the breath or a mantra. In this activity, the focal point is repetitive mark-making.

2. Demonstrate by making a small mark (a circle, dot, dash, or square) in the upper corner of a sticky note. Repeat the mark, creating a row of approximately 20 across.

3. Explain that each mark represents a new moment in time to observe and accept, just as it is. Clarify that accepting is not the same as liking.

4. Explain that your client will continue making rows of the same mark until the sticky note is full, with the goal of focusing on each new mark as it is made. Invite your client to begin when ready.

5. While your client draws, occasionally prompt them to return their focus to their mark-making: "If your mind has gotten distracted or wandered, notice that. Then, gently bring your attention back to each new mark you make."

6. Invite your client to place the completed sticky note on a blank piece of paper. Encourage them to create one meditative sticky note daily, using a different shape or mark. Add each completed sticky note to the paper, assembling a patchwork of present moments.

Discussion questions:

- Were you able to notice when your mind wandered or gave opinions about your marks? Were there any themes to your thoughts, such as planning, questioning, or criticizing?

- What feelings did you notice during this activity: bored, calm, tired, antsy?

- How might focusing on each present moment and accepting it just as it is help in real life? How might it help with anger?

Helpful tip: Challenge speedy clients to slow down their mark-making. Get curious about other times in their life they want to go fast, act quickly, or get something over with. Explore how practicing slowing down could be helpful in times of anger or frustration.

★ SELF-CARE DEDICATION DOODLE

Self-care need not involve extensive planning or timely commitments. Even simple acts like doodling (Isis *et al.* 2023) or gazing at the sky (Conwaya and Hefferonb 2019; Keltner 2023) decrease stress levels and put emotions in perspective. What self-care requires is dedication to occasionally prioritize personal welfare over tasks, even for a moment. This exercise is designed for the dual purpose of sparking immediate stress relief through spontaneous doodling while supporting long-term dedication to personal wellbeing.

Materials: Drawing paper (any paper works), drawing utensils (colored pencils, markers, or crayons)

1. Invite your client to write the phrase "Permission to self-care" in the center of their paper. Discuss how it feels to read this phrase.

2. Prompt your client to draw a decorative border around the phrase, using lines, dots, shapes, or symbols. Encourage your client to work spontaneously.

3. Invite your client to doodle another pattern around, or radiating out from, the first border. Encourage your client to use colors, lines, or symbols that convey pleasant feelings associated with self-care. They need not overthink it.

4. Prompt your client to create a third concentric pattern including shapes, symbols, or colors that reflect self-care activities such as books, clouds, mugs, stick people, or plants. These can be abstract or figurative.

5. Challenge your client to create a final pattern that captures practical self-care considerations. Dashes can symbolize length of time, moons or suns might represent times of day, words can specify days of the week, or symbols can convey locations.

6. Give permission to stop when your client feels it is complete.

Discussion questions:

- What was it like to work spontaneously? Do you tend to be spontaneous or organized with self-care in real life? How does that help or hinder you?

- What is the overall feeling of the completed drawing? What might that say about how you feel about self-care?

- What, if any, self-care interests did this activity inspire? Did the activity, itself, feel like self-care, or not?

Helpful tip: Some clients enjoy spontaneity whereas others benefit from more structure. If needed, increase structure by offering a template with pre-drawn concentric circles. Include written prompts for each circle, such as "free doodle," "self-care feelings," "self-care activities," and "practical planning."

★ SELF-SABOTAGE DIFFUSER

Excuses and self-criticism readily interfere with efforts to prioritize self-care. Sabotaging thoughts like these do not like to back down from an internal debate. They tend to get louder and more insistent when we counter them with encouraging thoughts. They prefer immediate gratification over long-term benefit, and can convince even highly motivated individuals to shirk the healthier option. Instead of fighting a losing argument, this acitivity teaches clients to directly transform sabotaging thoughts from outright convincing to utterly laughable.

Materials: Drawing paper (any paper works), drawing utensils (colored pencils, markers, or crayons)

1. Explain that adding silly elements to sabotaging thoughts diminishes their power by making them appear less true and persuasive.

2. Ask your client to imagine a self-care activity they would like to do more often.

3. Invite them to jot down all thoughts that come to mind when they think of doing the activity, including both motivating and discouraging thoughts.

4. Direct your client to choose one discouraging thought that regularly sabotages their self-care. Ask them to say it aloud.

5. Invite your client to write the thought prominently on a new piece of paper, making it appear as silly or outrageous as possible. For example, they might draw a ridiculous character saying the phrase, or write it in bold, pink, sparkly balloon letters.

6. Ask your client to imagine how the phrase would now sound if spoken from its new form. Would it sound like a cartoon character? Would it be menacing or meek? Invite your client to say the phrase in the altered voice a few times out loud or in their imagination.

Discussion questions:

- How did you feel about the thought before and after your drawing? Was there a change?

- What did you notice when you said the thought with an altered voice versus when you first said it in your normal voice?

- Is there any helpfulness in this thought, or is it always unhelpful? Under what conditions might it be helpful, if any?

Helpful tip: Help your client practice this activity entirely in their imagination so they can use this strategy anytime to disempower sabotaging thoughts. Invite your client to select a sabotaging thought, imagine it having a silly or outrageous form, and assign it a new voice to match.

★ HOPE HEIGHTENER

Hope reminds us that positive outcomes are possible. Without hope, anger can fester or become retaliatory instead of inspiring change. Hope is proactive, rather than reactive. It can get us unstuck and push us toward resolutions. Hope is healthy for the mind, body, and relationships (Long *et al.* 2020; Schornick *et al.* 2023). When we connect with hopeful thoughts and feelings, we are practicing self-care. Use this hope-activating activity to boost positive feelings and inspire the belief that things can get better.

Materials: Drawing paper (any paper works), drawing utensils (colored pencils, markers, or crayons)

1. Prompt your client to think of a real or imaginary place, animal, or person that evokes hopeful feelings.

2. Guide your client to use their imagination to zoom in on the details of that place, animal, or person, noticing how they feel inside as they do.

3. Ask your client to describe feelings and sensations that accompany hope, giving examples such as light, solid, wispy, warm, cool, energized, and relaxed.

4. Invite your client to imagine what their hopeful feeling would look like, if it had a color, texture, and form. Ask them to describe or draw it.

5. Prompt your client to imagine putting their hope under a magnifying glass to see more details. Invite them to describe or draw what they see now.

6. Ask your client to imagine where they would like to keep hope, like an imaginary box, grassy field, or their heart. Invite them to describe or add drawn details of the place directly onto their existing image of hope.

Discussion questions:

- Did it feel pleasant, unpleasant, or neutral to be in the presence of hope? Did you notice any downsides or risks associated with feeling hopeful?

- What was it like to magnify hope? Did anything surprise you, or not?

- What beliefs about yourself or your situation arise when you focus on your image of hope?

Helpful tip: Invite your client to pair a subtle movement with their image of hope in order to create another way to access hopeful feelings. Let the movement be spontaneous and arise from your client. Practice strengthening hope by prompting your client to reimagine their image while making their associated gesture or movement.

★ DIAGONAL BREATH

Breathwork is a well-established method for supporting internal balance, physical health, and mental clarity (Nestor 2020). From interrupting negative thought patterns to improving blood pressure, intentional breathing has both immediate and long-term benefits. Because recurrent anger takes a toll on the mind and body, breathwork is essential self-care. Use this activity in a pinch to support immediate emotional regulation, offer it regularly to strengthen emotional flexibility, and suggest it for between-session self-care maintenance.

Materials: Drawing paper (any kind), drawing or writing utensil

1. Explain that anger makes the breath quick and shallow. Intentional long, deep breaths return the body to a balanced state, where we can solve problems more effectively.

2. Model placing a drawing or writing utensil at the lower-left edge of a paper, near the corner. Inhale. On the exhale draw a diagonal line, ending at the bottom of the paper. Inhale to return the utensil back to the left edge, placing it slightly above the first line. Exhale to draw a diagonal, parallel line. Repeat, placing each new line slightly above the previous one.

3. Point out that the lines will lengthen as the drawing progresses toward the wider, center section. As the lines lengthen, so will the inhales and the exhales.

4. Provide options to create straight or wavy lines, or both. Remind clients to let their breath lead the drawing or writing utensil. Invite your client to begin on their own paper whenever they are ready.

5. As needed, guide your client to slow their drawing hand to match their breath, being particularly mindful at the corners, where the lines are short.

6. Monitor your client for signs of comfort or discomfort. Consider

pausing and checking in with how they are doing once they have reached the midway point of the paper.

Discussion questions:

- Did you experience any pleasant or unpleasant sensations during or after this activity? What parts were more pleasant? What parts were unpleasant?

- What was it like to coordinate your hand and your breath? How did it feel to make short lines versus long lines?

- How might this activity relate to the speed with which you move through your daily activities? Or the speed with which your thoughts change throughout the day?

Helpful tip: Clients with impaired attention, body discomfort, or those who are younger may struggle to complete an entire page of diagonals. Start with five diagonals, leaving large gaps in-between. Or invite clients to trace their hand instead of drawing diagonals. Prompt them to gradually inhale as they slowly trace each finger's incline and gradually exhale as they slowly trace each finger's decline.

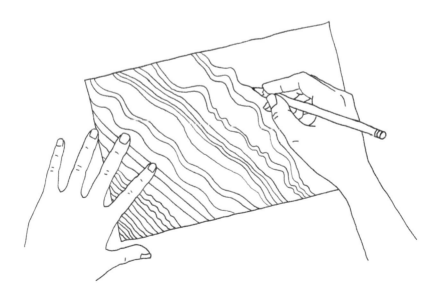

★ DISTRACTION DETECTOR

Distracting activities such as hobbies and social media provide needed breaks from intense thoughts and emotions. They can create space from stressful people and situations so challenges can be revisited with a clearer head. However, would-be helpful distractions can also unwittingly become unhealthy avoidance tactics. Use this activity to teach clients to detect avoidance tendencies and channel leisurely distractions into intentional acts of self-care.

Materials: Drawing paper (any paper works), drawing utensils (colored pencils, markers, or crayons)

1. Fold a piece of paper into three equal sections and then open it out.

2. Invite your client to draw a representation of stress in the center panel using images, shapes, scribbles, words, or colors. They may think of a specific stressor or what stress feels like in general.

3. Prompt your client to think of ways they distract themself from feeling stress, or habits they use to avoid dealing with potentially stressful situations.

4. Discuss how stress may momentarily decrease but then increase after prolonged avoidance. On the right-side panel, ask them to draw what stress looks like after prolonged avoidance.

5. Now ask your client to consider ways distraction can be used in a time-limited, intentional manner to help them feel refreshed and better prepared to address stressors.

6. On the left-side panel, ask your client to draw what stress would look like after time-limited, distracting activities used for rest and recovery rather than avoidance.

Discussion questions:

- Looking at your images, describe how stress is impacted differently by prolonged avoidance versus time-limited distraction. Are there any similarities?

- Pretend you were not the person who drew this. What might you wonder or guess about the person who created these images?

- How might you transform avoidance tactics into intentional, time-limited self-care in real life?

Helpful tip: If needed, make this activity more tangible by homing in on a specific stressor, avoidance tactic, or self-care alternative. Together, create labels for each panel, such as "Work stress" (center), "Stress after scrolling on social media for an hour" (right), "Stress after reading one book chapter" (left).

Chapter 2

GET TO KNOW ANGER

Anger is a basic, universally occurring emotion (Ekman 1992; Ekman and Cordaro 2011; Williams 2017). However, anger is experienced in many varied ways, including how long it takes to build up, how quickly it resolves, how intense it feels, and how it is expressed. Anger also differs in its individual purposes and origins. Add to that different beliefs about anger that impact our responses to it. While we share a general understanding of anger, it is truly individual. To influence anger, we cannot assume to understand what someone means when they say they "feel" angry. Instead, let us look closely at anger through a creative lens to discover its diverse, and sometimes unexpected, colors, textures, and forms.

This chapter will help you and your clients get deeply curious about anger's individual characteristics, regardless of whether they are anger-averse, anger-neutral, or quick-to-anger. It contains 10 creative activities to explore anger from diverse angles, including core characteristics, early signs, impact on sensations and thoughts, helpful functions, and more. The activities in this chapter also provide the added benefit of increasing objective distance from anger so clients learn to trust their ability to safely interact with and gain insight from anger. Reuse activities to examine anger's unique manifestations relative to different triggers, or to assess client progress over time.

★ ANGER'S DOORWAY

Anger can feel overwhelming. Even when anger is a welcomed sign of improved self-confidence or healthy empowerment, anger can create physical discomfort, agitation, or shutdown. Even clients capable of comfortably talking about anger may, in fact, be detaching from it and become flooded when practitioners urge them to feel, rather than think about, their anger. As such, it is prudent to get to know anger gradually so clients can learn to trust their ability to handle anger's presence.

Materials: Drawing paper (any paper works), drawing utensils (colored pencils, markers, or crayons), tape or a stapler

1. Explain that before examining anger, your client will create a door to keep anger behind. They will control when the door opens or closes, and by how much.

2. Fold a piece of paper in half to represent a door that can open and close. Orient the paper's fold on your client's left, the open flap to the right. Keep the paper folded shut so the door is closed.

3. Invite your client to imagine their door's details including materials, colors, and decorations. Ask if it would have a lock, doorknob, peep hole, sign, and welcome mat, or not? Invite your client to design the door using their drawing utensils.

4. Ask if your client would like to seal the door shut with tape or a stapler, or if they would prefer to leave it as is.

5. Once finished, invite your client to look at their door. Ask what it is like to imagine anger on the other side of the door.

6. Invite your client to make additions or changes so the door feels optimally secure.

Discussion questions:

- How do you feel when looking at this door, knowing that anger is behind it? What would it feel like to approach this door?

- How could you use this door to control anger's presence? What do you imagine you will discover on the other side of the door?

- How might your door image help you in real life when you sense anger?

Helpful tip: Art-averse clients may prefer imagining a door rather than making one. Guide your client to close their eyes or leave them open if they prefer. Follow the same activity steps, asking for descriptions of what they visualize.

★ BOTTLED-UP ANGER

Clients may feel anger intensely or bottle it up quickly, numbing to anger's presence before they are aware it exists. Either scenario calls for a gentle approach to gathering first impressions of anger so that clients maintain a sense of control and security throughout the process of getting familiar with anger. This activity honors the protective function of "bottling up emotions" while reducing harmful suppression so clients can allow anger to safely float into awareness.

Materials: Drawing paper (any paper works), drawing utensils (colored pencils, markers, or crayons)

1. Explain that this activity will help your client gather first impressions of anger in a gentle, controlled manner.

2. Invite your client to imagine a transparent or translucent container that holds anger. It may contain a subtler form of anger, like frustration or agitation. Provide examples like a glass bottle, lava lamp, or plasticware container.

3. Invite your client to draw their container. Suggest that your client consider its size in addition to its shape. Remind your client that there is no right or wrong answer.

4. Ask your client if they can comfortably imagine their angry feelings coming into view within the container. If not, look ahead to the helpful tip for this activity. If yes, continue to step five.

5. Invite your client to add colors, shapes, lines, symbols, or words that represent anger or other types of angry feelings inside the container.

6. Ask your client if they would like to add anything outside the container.

Discussion questions:

- Is your container an adequate shape, material, and size for its contents? Is there anything you would change about your container after having added symbols of anger?

- Describe what you drew inside the container. What do you wonder about anger based on the colors, shapes, lines, symbols or words you used?

- What would it be like to imagine taking an even closer look inside?

Helpful tip: If your client shows or reports discomfort, invite them to imagine the container as far away as needed to tolerate its presence, like across the street, in another country, or even on another planet. Invite them to redraw the container small enough to demonstrate its distance away before adding the images of anger within.

★ CANDID ANGER PORTRAIT

The simple, tried-and-true art therapy directive, "Show me what that looks like," guides clients to transform emotions into visual forms. However, some clients may not be able to envision anger so readily. Discomfort with anger, dissociation, self-judgment, visual-learning weakness, over-intellectualization, or unease with art-making can all pose challenges to the creative process in therapy. This activity provides gentle guidance for not-so-quick-to-create clients so that they, too, can benefit from constructing a candid portrait of anger.

Materials: Drawing paper (any paper works), drawing utensils (colored pencils, markers, or crayons)

1. Explain that your client is going to imagine that anger has its own physical appearance, opinions, and behaviors.

2. Encourage spontaneity by setting this scene: "Imagine meeting anger for the first time. I open the door and anger walks in. Without overthinking, what do you see come into the room?"

3. Simplify if needed. Ask what color your client imagines. Next, ask what shape anger has. Invite your client to draw a shape, scribble, or other form in their chosen color.

4. Invite your client to imagine where anger would spend most of its time. It can be abstract or recognizable. Ask your client to add an environment.

5. Encourage adding details or objects to tell a story, such as what anger enjoys doing, what it eats, who it hangs out with, what it dislikes, or what it feels passionate about. Remind your client that it is okay if answers seem nonsensical.

6. Ask your client if they would like to title this portrait of anger.

Discussion questions:

- What does this image tell you about anger? What does it not tell you about anger?

- If your portrait of anger could speak, what would it say about the current situation with which you are dealing?

- How long do you imagine anger has been working hard at its job? Is there anything it would rather be doing?

Helpful tip: Some clients require more literal options to help them visualize anger. Offer a menu of emojis to choose from. Or invite your client to create a word portrait by writing the word "anger" using a color, size, and font that convey anger's qualities and characteristics.

★ ANGER ADVISOR

Emotions are like personal advisors. They report on the status of relationships, work, and leisure. They provide feedback about strengths and weaknesses, and give opinions about how to handle opportunities and threats. Emotions mean well. However, their advice is not always entirely beneficial. This activity helps clients appreciate anger's role as an advisor, and not as the boss. It allows clients to practice listening to anger with both the distance and intention needed to discern helpful, non-reactive action.

Materials: Drawing paper (any paper works), drawing utensils (colored pencils, markers, or crayons)

1. Explain that anger is like an overactive advisor that strongly influences our actions, reactions, or inaction. Our task is to decipher and thoughtfully consider its advice before acting.

2. Invite your client to make a scribble to represent anger's energy. Prompt them to consider anger's size, speed, and intensity. It may start slow, and then build its energy. It may be a small, dense scribble, or an explosive scribble that consumes most of the page.

3. Ask, "If this scribble could talk, what would it say?" Allow the spontaneous addition of words (see the helpful tip for a contra-indication consideration).

4. Deepen the dialogue with anger by prompting your client to imagine asking the scribble meaningful questions, such as "Why are you working so hard?" "What are you protecting me from?" "What do you want me to know?"

5. After you ask one question, pause to allow your client to write down an answer from anger's point of view. Then ask a new question.

6. Remind clients not to ignore automatic thoughts in answer to

questions, even if they seem nonsensical or irrelevant. They may have hidden meaning.

Discussion questions:

- What did you learn about anger from your scribble drawing?

- How might anger's input help you? How might it not help you?

- What might happen if anger didn't work so hard? Consider both the positive and the negatives.

Helpful tip: When anger is allowed to speak spontaneously without the structure of questions, it may curse or say unkind things. Depending on where you are and on the age of the clients with whom you work, you may choose to skip step three and go straight to the meaningful dialogue prompts in step four.

★ ANGER'S COMICAL CREW

Subtler angry emotions often precede stronger ones. However, not all angry feelings are merely different intensities of the same emotion. Anger, annoyance, resentment, displeasure, frustration, outrage, and impatience may belong to the same family of feelings, but they are distinct experiences that come with different preferences and desires. Use this activity's comical approach to exaggerate differences between related emotions so clients can shed light on the distinct needs of their angry crew.

Materials: Drawing paper (any paper works), drawing utensils (colored pencils, markers, or crayons), a device to search online (optional)

1. Explain that your client is going to explore variations of angry emotions by exaggerating their differences. Provide examples of angry emotions such as those in the introduction to this activity.

2. Ask your client to choose an angry emotion they have experienced recently or feel often. Invite them to draw a cartoon representation and label it with the feeling word.

3. Provide creative support by showing online examples of simple cartoon faces or funny-shape people cartoons.

4. Ask what other angry emotions your client experiences (or witnesses in others). Prompt them to draw a new representative cartoon and label it.

5. Continue guiding your client to add additional cartoon characters until a range of three to five angry emotions is represented.

6. Prompt your client to consider what each emotion needs. Invite your client to add one, two, or three words near each character to indicate what they need or desire.

Discussion questions:

- What similarities or differences do you notice between the different characters and their needs? Which characters stand out to you?

- Do any of these characters work together or help each other?

- What would happen if any of these characters were bigger? What would happen if any of them were smaller?

Helpful tip: Simplify this activity if needed. Instead of drawing cartoons, prompt your client to draw exaggerated shapes that correspond with their different angry emotions. Ask, "If annoyance (rage, irritation, impatience, frustration) was a shape, what shape would it be?" Ask clients to draw one shape for each emotion, considering size and placement on the page.

★ LANDSCAPE OF ANGER

Anger is commonly compared to a volcano because of its explosive power, to an iceberg because of what hides beneath, or to fire because it lingers and harms. However, many common analogies are unsuitable or inadequate to describe individual experiences of anger. Anger builds, peaks, and resolves with varied durations, intensities, and intervals. What comes before anger and what remains after is different between individuals and incidences. This activity broadens the use of nature as a metaphor so clients can familiarize themselves with their own unique, internal landscape of anger.

Materials: Drawing paper, images of nature (from magazines or online), scissors, glue stick, paper, drawing utensils (optional)

1. Explain that your client is going to create a landscape containing images representing different stages of anger.

2. Invite your client to look through images of nature including animals, weather, plants, elements, and ecosystems.

3. Ask your client to select and cut out images of nature to represent stages of anger including before, increase, peak, resolution, and after.

4. Give examples like, "Before anger, it feels like a desert. Anger increasing is like an oak tree. Anger at its peak is like a cloudy sky. Anger's resolution is like rain. And after is like plants sprouting."

5. Invite your client to arrange and glue selected images onto a landscape scene.

6. Optionally invite your client to draw additional features or details to complete their image.

Discussion questions:

- Tell me about your images. How would you describe the different elements? How does each element impact the overall image?

- Which parts of your landscape feel positive, negative, or neutral to you?

- If you were to enter this landscape, where would you place yourself? Which part would be easiest or most difficult to be in?

Helpful tip: Ask local libraries for free, outdated nature magazines. If you cannot access magazines or printed images, share online images to inspire an anger landscape drawing instead. Assist art-shy clients by offering to sketch images they select. Ask where and how large to sketch each image.

★ EARLY MESSAGES MANDALA

Influence from caregivers, peers, community members, and the media is powerful. Observations and interactions not only impact our conscious opinions about anger; relationships throughout life also influence our automatic feelings about, reactions to, and expression of, anger. Illuminating these unconscious messages is a key component to getting to know anger and ultimately changing unhealthy patterns. This activity brings awareness to early messages about anger so clients can choose beliefs that serve them well and rewrite those that do not.

Materials: Drawing paper (any paper works), drawing utensils (colored pencils, markers, or crayons)

1. Draw four concentric rings on a piece of paper, or print out the image provided below.

2. Label each ring as follows: middle: "home"; second: "peers"; third: "outside adults/community"; final: "world/media."

3. Ask your client to consider messages they have received about anger from each area. Ask adults to think back to their childhood and adolescence. Ask children and teens to consider current influences. Explain that messages about anger may be clearly stated, subtly implied, or observable in others' behaviors.

4. Discuss examples of messages, such as "Anger is scary," "It's not okay to express anger," "Anger is part of love," and "People listen when you're angry." Invite your client to write a relevant message in each ring.

5. Invite your client to add lines, shapes, colors, or patterns to convey their experience of anger, or absence of anger, in each ring. Remind clients there may be conflicting experiences in a single ring.

6. Provide more structure by limiting options, if needed. For example,

suggest using colors only to represent the presence and intensity of anger in each ring.

Discussion questions:

- What do you notice, looking at the drawing as a whole? What rings stand out to you?

- How might these experiences have influenced ways you respond to anger today? How have they impacted your responses to others' anger?

- Which messages have helped you, and how? Which messages have hindered you? How would you rewrite those messages if you could?

Helpful tip: Learn more by asking your client to select one message or ring that was most influential. Ask, "If we zoomed in on this one ring, what more would we see?" Prompt your client to create a separate drawing.

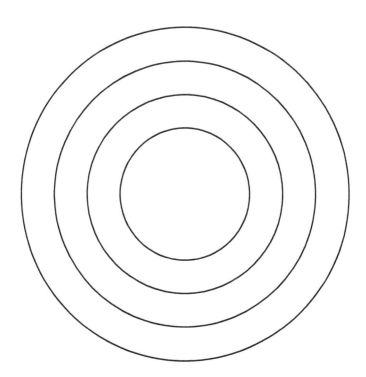

★ MIND–BODY BONDS

The mind and body are in constant communication. Thoughts cue the body to shift emotions as well as alter muscle tension, heart and breath rate, temperature, digestion, and more. These moment-to-moment bodily changes, in turn, send messages back to the brain, influencing beliefs about the past, present, and future. Therefore, getting to know anger, in part, involves becoming familiar with our own experience of this mind–body feedback loop. In this activity, clients will learn to pay attention to internal cues of anger, both in the mind and body, so they can explore options for altering the cycle.

Materials: Drawing paper (any paper works), drawing utensils (colored pencils, markers, or crayons)

1. Draw a large oval on one side of the paper and an upright rectangle on the opposite side. Explain that the oval is the brain and the rectangle is the body. Optionally, alter basic shapes to resemble a brain and torso more closely.

2. Explain the mind–body feedback loop. Provide specific examples of how thoughts influence bodily sensations and functions and bodily sensations impact thoughts.

3. Prompt your client to remember a situation that angered them. As they vividly recall the situation, ask them to notice changes in their thoughts and bodily sensations.

4. If your client does not notice changes in the present moment, ask them to remember any thoughts or physical sensations they experienced at the time. Offer examples of thoughts or sensations that commonly accompany anger, if needed.

5. Direct your client to fill in the brain (oval) with lines, shapes, colors, images, or words to represent thoughts. Direct your client to fill in the body (rectangle), with lines, shapes, colors, images, or words to represent emotions and sensations.

6. Invite your client to draw several connecting lines between the brain and body to represent lines of communication.

Discussion questions:

- Was it easier to fill in the image of the brain (oval) or the body (rectangle)? Why do you think that is?

- What do you notice about the relationship between the image of the brain and the image of the body?

- How would altering the body change the brain? How might altering the brain change the body? What would you add or take away from one to change the other?

Helpful tip: Expand on this activity by inviting your client to create an environment showing external factors that trigger anger. Prompt clients to represent the event from step three, or add lines, shapes, colors, images, or words representing as many triggers as they can think of.

★ SEISMIC TRIGGERS

An important part of getting to know anger is getting to know triggers to anger. Examining triggers reveals patterns in the types of situations that are particularly bothersome. And because triggers tend to repeat themselves, we have ample opportunity to evaluate our reactions and prepare to respond differently in the future. In this activity, clients will acknowledge a variety of maddening situations along with the angry energy they evoke. Use it to uncover patterns in what sparks anger as well as tendencies to over- or under-react.

Materials: Drawing paper (any paper works), scratch paper, pencil, black marker

1. Seismometers measure earthquake intensity by translating vibrational energy into jagged lines. Explain that your client will similarly portray angry energy in line drawings.

2. Invite your client to brainstorm situations, people, places, or thoughts that anger them. Write these on scratch paper.

3. Ask your client to orient a piece of drawing paper vertically. Prompt your client to vividly recall one trigger they identified. Encourage them to focus on the sensations and intensity of anger when they think of this trigger.

4. Instruct your client to energetically draw a line from left to right, moving their pencil up and down like a seismometer, to mimic the quality and intensity of their felt anger. Remind clients that anger intensity may be high, even if they don't outwardly express it. Ask the client to label the line with the trigger.

5. Invite the client to repeat step four with each trigger, drawing a new seismogram line above or beneath the previous one. Offer creative options such as using waves, loop-the-loops, or sharp up-and-down motions to show variability in angry energy.

6. Once all the triggers are translated into lines, invite your client to slowly and deliberately trace the lines with a black marker.

Discussion questions:

- Do you notice any patterns between the lines? Are there similarities between the types of triggers that produced those lines?

- What was it like to energetically draw the various lines? What was it like to trace the lines more slowly and deliberately with the black marker?

- Do any of the lines show energy that appears out of proportion to the trigger? Is the energy higher or lower than you might expect for that trigger?

Helpful tip: If clients struggle to identify triggers, help by asking if they have ever experienced one of these common anger-inducing situations: unfairness, boundary-crossing, over-stimulation, blocked goals, being unacknowledged, feeling disrespected, or having unmet needs.

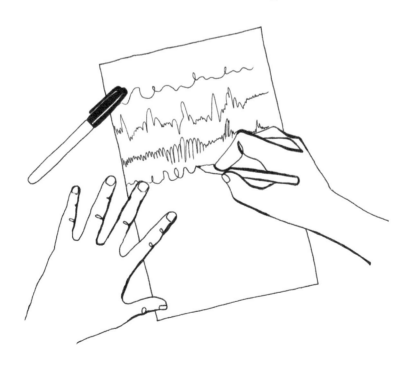

★ ANGER'S CORE

What angers us is often more complex than it appears. While events and angry responses are often observable, what we don't see are the rapid automatic and cascading thoughts that further provoke and compound anger. Sometimes it is not the external incident so much as the internal, often distorted belief about the event that prompts outrage. This activity unearths layers of negative thoughts so we can get to know anger at its core. Clients may be surprised to learn that their anger has less to do with the situation and more to do with false beliefs about themselves.

Materials: Assorted-color construction paper, glue stick, pen

1. Explain that your client will create a collage representing layers of hidden beliefs that impact anger. Use the analogy of the invisible layers of earth beneath the surface.

2. Ask your client to tell you about a specific anger-inducing situation. As they do, invite them to slowly rip long, wide strips of different-colored construction paper.

3. Invite your client to glue one strip horizontally onto the upper portion of an intact piece of paper. This first strip represents the earth's surface. Ask what is on the surface of anger. On the strip, prompt them to write and complete the sentence "I'm angry because…"

4. Prompt your client to glue a second horizontal strip beneath and overlapping the prior strip. Ask, "What does that make you think, even if you know it isn't true?" Ask them to write the belief on the new strip.

5. Repeat step four several more times, each time referencing the prior statement and asking, "What does that make you think, even if you know it isn't true?" Here is an example: (1) I am angry because my friend cancelled plans. (2) I think that is rude.

(3) Which makes me think they don't care about me as much as I care about them.

6. On the final strip, ask, "What does that make you think about *yourself*, even if you know it isn't true?" The example in step five might conclude with, "Which means I'm not important." Prompt you client to write the core negative belief on the final strip.

Discussion questions:

- What was it like to do this activity? Did anything surprise you?

- Is there a story behind any of these beliefs? Do they remind you of other times or situations?

- Think about the different layers of the earth's crust. What images or details might you add to each of these layers to show changing materials, temperature, or other elements?

Helpful tip: Identifying negative core beliefs can be difficult. Assist by providing examples of what some people might believe, such as: "It's my fault," "I'm not capable," "I'm not okay," "I'm not trustworthy," "I'm not in control." Emphasize that people can *feel* these are true even if they *know* they are not.

Chapter 3

RECRUIT OTHER EMOTIONS

Anger does not operate alone. The internal world is a complex system of multiple emotions, each with their own needs, opinions, and urges. Anger may be responsible for banishing unwanted emotions, thoughts, and memories. Or it may partner with other emotions to motivate change. Anger may have assumed too much leadership of the internal world, or it may be underactive. Like a member of a team, anger is impacted by its role and responsibilities as well as the trust and comradery it has with its teammates. To influence anger, it is vital to consider its place within the network of all emotions working to support each person.

This chapter contains 10 creative activities that examine how other emotions spark, collaborate with, or hide beneath, anger. You will find activities to untangle co-occurring emotions, uncover masked emotions, activate alternative energizing emotions, and more. This chapter also offers opportunities to differentiate between transient emotions and enduring values that make up one's core self. Each activity, in its own way, supports the higher goal of developing a healthier role for anger within the larger, internal world.

★ EMOTION UNTANGLE

Emotions are more complex than the words we have for expressing them. Not only are emotions nuanced, but we also generally lack a vocabulary that describes the common experience of feeling several emotions at once. When clients describe feeling overwhelmed or confused, or if they report not knowing how they feel, it is often because more than one emotion is at work. This creative activity builds foundational skills for naming co-occurring emotions, and learning that even seemingly contradictory emotions can co-exist harmoniously.

Materials: Drawing paper (any paper works), drawing utensils (colored pencils, markers, or crayons), sticky notes (optional)

1. Initiate this activity when your client struggles to identify, feels overwhelmed with, or is confused by, emotions. Or invite your client to recall a time they experienced many emotions at once.

2. Ask your client to select one color to represent each identifiable emotion. If they cannot yet identify separate emotions, invite them to randomly choose several colors.

3. Invite your client to scribble with each color, overlapping others to show how entangled they are. Suggest your client represent the quality, size, and intensity of each emotion within the tangle.

4. Now it is time to untangle the emotions. Challenge your client to find the end of one colored scribble. Prompt them to lengthen the line until it reaches a blank space on the page. Here, ask them to add a small, distinct scribble or shape in that color.

5. Repeat step four for each color. Ask your client to label emotions they can name.

6. Optionally invite your client to optionally write the word "and" around the paper, to acknowledge that separate emotions can co-exist.

Discussion questions:

- What is it like looking at the entangled colors? What feeling do you get? What was it like to separate each color?

- Let's name each emotion or color you felt, using the word "and." For example, "I felt yellow *and* brown *and* green *and*..." or "I felt tired *and* disappointed *and* frustrated..." What do you notice when you do this?

- In real life, it is easier to separate and identify emotions after taking space from the triggering person or situation. What are some practical ways you might take space, either physically or mentally?

Helpful tip: Clients may need extra space to separate colors if the entangled scribble fills the whole paper. Expand available space by attaching one sticky note for each color around the edge. Alternatively, tape a new piece of paper to the side.

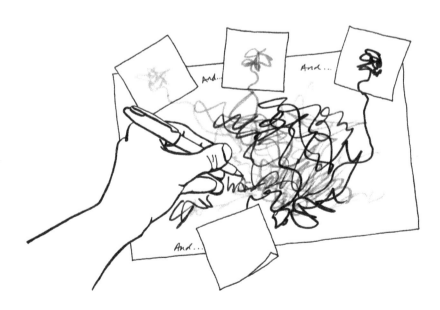

★ SIMULTANEOUS SENSATIONS

We constantly experience different sensations throughout the body. The tongue in our mouth has a different sensation than our feet on the floor or the hair on our neck. We necessarily tune out most sensations until we experience something intense, uncomfortable, or unfamiliar. Then that is all we feel. Therefore, it is important to learn how to intentionally shift gears. This activity promotes awareness of simultaneous sensations, so clients can learn to change focus from signs of turmoil to soothing sensations.

Materials: Drawing paper (any paper works), drawing utensils (colored pencils, markers, or crayons)

1. Fold a piece of paper multiple times into a square. Unfold to reveal approximately 12 to 16 equal sections.

2. Invite your client to bring their attention to any bodily sensation they notice. If they need help, suggest noticing their feet on the floor or rubbing fabric with their fingers. Or if they feel angry and are comfortable doing so, suggest noticing sensations resulting from anger. Provide common examples, such as muscle tension, increased heart rate, or sweaty hands.

3. Guide your client to focus on and describe sensations they feel in that body part or region. Provide examples such as warm, cool, tense, open, relaxed, tingly, painful, heavy, and light.

4. Ask your client to draw or write the body part in one section.

5. Prompt your client to add colors, lines, shapes, symbols, or patterns in the corresponding section to express types and qualities of sensations felt there.

6. Repeat steps two through five with a different part of the body until all, or several, sections are filled in. If your client focuses exclusively on unpleasant sensations, challenge them to seek a neutral or pleasant sensation.

Discussion questions:

- What was it like to notice pleasant or neutral sensations? What happened when you focused on unpleasant sensations?

- Looking at your image, what do you notice about the individual parts? Now hold the paper at arm's length. What do you notice about the whole?

- How does the intensity of one sensation change when focusing on another sensation? How might shifting your attention to pleasant or neutral sensations help when you feel angry?

Helpful tip: If your client struggles to notice sensations, invite them to activate three obvious sensations, like tapping feet, wiggling fingers, and swaying. Give them the humorous challenge of doing all three motions at once while shifting their attention from one sensation to another. Using a piece of paper folded into three sections, invite your client to express the quality of each sensation using colors, lines, shapes, symbols, or patterns.

★ VULNERABILITY CLOAK

Anger sometimes protects against experiencing vulnerable emotions like loneliness, regret, and shame. Not only does anger's empowering energy feel better; it can also prevent the onset of depression, withdrawal, and hopelessness that could interfere with day-to-day functioning. Without anger, some may struggle to get out of bed. Yet without acknowledging vulnerable emotions, core therapeutic needs go unaddressed. This activity gently acknowledges emotions cloaked by anger while giving clients control to keep anger securely intact.

Materials: Drawing paper (any paper works), drawing utensils (colored pencils, markers, or crayons), glue stick, tape, or rubber band (optional)

1. Cut or tear a long strip of paper approximately one to two inches wide. Show your client how to fold the strip accordion-style four or more times.

2. Keep the accordion strip folded so only the top surface shows. Ask your client to use colors, lines, shapes, words, or symbols to represent anger on the top.

3. Ask your client to open the top fold to reveal a blank section. Invite your client to use colors, lines, shapes, words, or symbols to represent a vulnerable feeling they might experience if they were not feeling angry. Offer examples such as hurt, weak, sad, disappointed.

4. Ask your client to close that flap and open the next, blank section. Invite your client to use colors, lines, shapes, words, or symbols to represent another vulnerable feeling they might experience. For example, say, "And if you felt sad, then what more might you feel?" Offer more suggestions such as lonely, ridiculous, empty, hopeless.

5. Continue this process until your client is finished, even if the strip is not filled in.

6. Invite your client to fold the strip back into its original, stacked accordion, with anger visible on the top and vulnerable feelings hidden.

Discussion questions:

- What was this activity like for you? Was anything difficult or uncomfortable?

- What is it like to unfold the accordion? What is it like to fold it back up?

- Choose one vulnerable feeling that is tolerable to look at. Open to that section. What would this feeling need to feel better? What would you say to a friend who was having this feeling?

Helpful tip: Some clients benefit from exercising additional control at the end of this activity to ensure vulnerable emotions are secured away. Optionally, invite your client to seal the accordion paper shut with a glue stick, tape, or rubber band. Or invite them to seal it in an envelope.

★ COMPASSIONATE COMPARISON

Our internal world is rich with emotional resources that can help us soothe, activate, or helpfully harness anger. However, these resources are not easily accessed without practice, especially when anger tends toward negativity, criticism, and blame. Compassion is one well-documented emotion with promising potential to buffer anger by increasing other perspective-taking and pleasant feelings as well as creating long-term structural changes in the brain, paving a pathway for other positive emotions (Förster and Kanske 2021, 2022). This activity awakens compassion, compares it with criticism, and guides clients to deliberate on the more desirable direction.

Materials: Drawing paper (any paper works), black pen

1. Ask your client to squeeze their fist, and then to relax it. Explain that it is easier to observe differences between tense and relaxed with direct comparison, and that this activity similarly compares criticism and compassion.

2. Fold a piece of paper into four sections. Invite your client to consider times they had critical or judgmental thoughts about others. Or initiate this activity when you observe your client making critical or blaming remarks.

3. Ask your client to use abstract lines, shapes, or images in the first panel to illustrate the impact of critical or judgmental thoughts on their emotions and actions.

4. Repeat steps two and three, prompting your client to consider times their mind made self-critical or self-blaming thoughts. Add these to the second panel.

5. For the third panel, repeat steps two and three, focusing on kind, loving, or forgiving thoughts toward another. Let your client know it's okay to think of a person or animal about whom it is easy to have kind, loving, or forgiving thoughts.

6. For the fourth panel, repeat steps two and three, focusing on times your client experienced kind, loving, or forgiving thoughts toward themself.

Discussion questions:

- Looking at your image, how do compassionate experiences compare or contrast with critical experiences? Which drawing would you like to spend more time in?

- Was it easier to draw critical or compassionate feelings? Was it easier to draw about others or yourself?

- Using your images of compassion, how might you describe what compassion is to someone who is unfamiliar with the emotion? How might you explain the helpfulness of compassion in daily life?

Helpful tip: If clients struggle to think of personal experiences, prompt them to think of times they felt critical or loving toward an animal, stranger, or television character instead. Explain that any of these figures are merely access points to awaken something that exists within your client. If they can feel compassionate toward an animal, for example, they can learn to extend that feeling to themself and to others.

★ FOREGROUND FEELINGS

Anger has advantages such as increased feelings of control, courage, and self-assuredness. Because of this, some clients may intentionally or unconsciously resist strategies to soothe anger for fear they will lose empowering feelings as well. This activity shows clients that empowerment need not go hand in hand with anger. It helps clients amplify positive, uplifting emotions by placing them in the foreground while allowing anger to fade into the background.

Materials: Drawing paper (any paper works), pencil, three shades of the same-colored drawing utensil (such as dark blue, mid-range blue, and light blue)

1. Discuss desirable emotions your client feels when angered, such as control, power, motivation, or courage. Explain that your client will practice detaching empowering emotions from anger by playing with perspective.

2. Describe perspective in terms of foreground, middle ground, and background. Demonstrate by drawing a tree in the foreground, flowers in the middle ground, and mountains in the background. Remind your client this is only an example and that they may use different symbols and words.

3. Emphasize that foreground objects are large, bold, detailed, and dark whereas background objects are small, light, and lack detail.

4. Invite your client to select three shades of the same color to represent foreground, middle ground, and background.

5. Prompt your client to draw bold, decorative, detailed words or symbols of empowered emotions in the foreground and middle ground. Remind your client to use the darker two colors.

6. Invite your client to add a small, hazy word or symbol of anger in the far background, using the lightest color.

Discussion questions:

- What was it like to separate empowered emotions from anger? In what ways was it difficult, or easy?

- Can you think of times you felt empowered without anger? When do you think anger and empowerment became intertwined?

- Do you think it is possible to feel empowered emotions without as much anger in real life? What do you see in your image that tells you that?

Helpful tip: If time allows, ask your client to first draw anger in the foreground and empowering emotions in the background. Then, prompt a separate drawing where anger is moved to the background and empowering emotions are brought into the foreground. Compare and contrast the two drawings as well as the feelings they evoke.

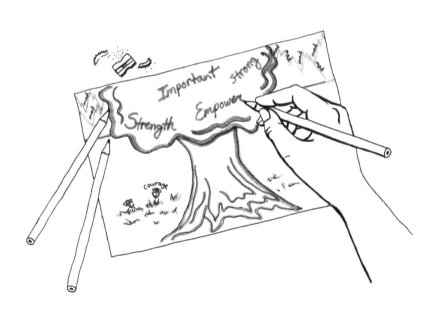

★ BALANCED BOXES

When we are in a balanced state, we have enough energy to handle daily tasks with enough calm to remain clear-headed and at ease. When anger or agitation increases energy, we may need relaxing activities to restore calm. If we have too little energy to address challenges, we may need an energetic boost to avoid becoming lethargic or uncaring. Sometimes recruiting other emotions involves accessing energetic or calming experiences to maintain, or regain, balance. This activity helps clients observe energy unevenness and consider ways to regain equilibrium.

Materials: Drawing paper (any paper works), pencil, ruler, black marker, drawing utensils (colored pencils, markers, or crayons)

1. Invite your client to use a pencil and ruler to draw one horizontal and two vertical lines across any part of their paper. Prompt your client to add more horizontal and vertical lines, either crossing or beginning and ending at existing lines.

2. Invite your client to thicken lines with a black marker.

3. Explain that your client will color boxes to show how energized or calm they felt recently.

4. Ask your client to select two colors they believe are energizing and two they believe are calming.

5. Ask if your client has felt more energized or calm recently. Direct your client to color larger boxes, and a greater percentage of boxes, with the color representing their dominant experience.

6. Prompt your client to color smaller and fewer boxes with the color representing their less dominant experience.

Discussion questions:

- In what ways does your overall image appear balanced or imbalanced? How might you adjust your image to show more balance?

- How does anger influence your energy level? What practical activities can shift your level of energy into a more balanced state?

- In what ways do energy and calm both help you? In what ways do they not?

Helpful tip: Sometimes it is enjoyable to have a period of more high-energy or low-energy experiences. Sometimes it gets in the way. Expand on this activity by asking your client to select four different colors representing: pleasant high energy, unpleasant high energy, pleasant low energy, and unpleasant low energy.

★ FEELING FUNDAMENTALS

Exploring emotions through art may be intuitive for some and difficult for others. For starters, identifying emotions requires complex skills that not everyone was taught or has exercised. While therapeutic art-making supports emotional intelligence skills, clients unaccustomed to thinking and communicating through visual, tactile, and sensory-motor means may feel stumped. Regardless of age or developmental level, many clients will benefit from focusing on the fundamentals of creatively recruiting other emotions. Use this activity to get back to basics while delivering a big therapeutic impact.

Materials: Drawing utensils (colored pencils, markers, or crayons)

1. Display a set of drawing utensils with a variety of colors. Invite your client to sort them into pleasant, unpleasant, and neutral (neither pleasant nor unpleasant) colors. Use alternative words that work for your client such as "like, don't like, indifferent" or "yes, nope, okay."

2. Invite your client to now sort each of the three piles into energizing, calming, or energy neutral.

3. Explain that your client will choose any situation, interaction, or activity that stood out from this past week. They will narrow in on a color that best represents how they felt during that situation.

4. Guide your client to describe the situation and identify if they felt pleasant, unpleasant, or neutral. Gesture to the corresponding colors.

5. Ask your client if their energy felt up, down, or in the middle during this situation.

6. Prompt your client to select a final color or colors that best represents their feeling about the situation.

Discussion questions:

- Was it difficult to know how you felt about each color during the initial sorting? Or did you know right away if a color was pleasant, unpleasant, calming, energizing, or neutral?

- What cues did you get from your mind and body about whether a color was pleasant or unpleasant? What cues did you get from your mind and body about whether a color calmed or energized you?

- Did you find more pleasant, unpleasant, or neutral colors? Did you find more energizing, calming, or energy-neutral colors? Does that reflect how you often feel in your life, or not?

Helpful tip: Provide examples of ways the mind and body give us information about likes, dislikes, and energy shifts. For example, we may smile or frown, sit taller or slump, notice our chest rise or sink, feel allured or repulsed, notice our eyes widen or droop, or observe our thoughts asking for more or less.

★ FINDING HOME BASE

Emotions inform important aspects of ourselves, but we are not our emotions. When connected with our core self, we observe objectively, creatively, and compassionately. Rather than impulsively reacting, we draw from emotions for self-discovery and improvement. We are also more able to align our behavior with personal and relationship goals and values. However, it is easy to lose sight of ourselves in the presence of strong, persistent emotions like anger. This activity helps clients define and establish their core self as a home base from which they can observe, rather than get swept up in, emotions.

Materials: Drawing paper (any paper works), drawing utensils (colored pencils, markers, or crayons)

1. Explain that while emotions inform who we are, including cares, worries, likes, and dislikes, we are not our emotions.

2. Invite your client to write their name, or a nickname, in the center of their paper. Emphasize that it is important to choose a name they strongly identify with and feel positive about. If need be, your client can write "me."

3. Prompt your client to be thoughtful when choosing the font, size, and color for their name.

4. Ask your client to embellish their name with images, symbols, or patterns that represent core components of who they are. These can include important values, ethics, roles, identities, cultures, family legacies, and spiritual beliefs.

5. Discuss how the resulting image can represent your client's home base, from which they can observe, encounter, and interact with other emotions.

6. Prompt your client to brainstorm emotions they experience in any given day. Invite them to write these around the rest of their paper.

Discussion questions:

- What was it like to spend time writing and decorating your name? How does it reflect who you are?

- What does your overall image convey about differences between who you are and what you feel?

- Do any of these emotions strongly inform who you are? Are there any emotions that you sometimes confuse with your core self?

Helpful tip: Some clients may want help translating acitivities (what I do) into deeper, core attibutes (who I am). Ask questions like, "What about this activity is important to you?" "How does it relate to what matters to you?" Or "What core part of yourself is active during this activity?" For example "I like to swim" may also mean they care about health and fitness or feel carefree and connected while in the water.

★ FAST FUNCTIONAL FEELINGS

Feelings often function with short-term goals in mind. They help us quickly approach or avoid situations without necessarily considering long-term consequences. Because of this, even if immediate needs are met, valuable energy, relationships, or opportunities may be jeopardized in the long run. This activity helps clients understand emotions' most basic impulses to seek or avoid. It can reveal go-to patterns and open options to recruit future-focused emotions to help balance out emotions that tend to function fast.

Materials: Drawing paper (any paper works), drawing utensils (colored pencils, markers, or crayons)

1. Help your client trace around both hands. Prompt your client to place one hand palm up, fingers spread and the other hand palm down, fingers together.

2. Explain that most emotions urge people to either seek or avoid something. In this activity the open palm is ready to receive and represents seeking. The hand with closed fingers resembles a stop gesture and represents avoiding.

3. Discuss a time your client experienced a strong, basic emotion like anger, sadness, happiness, fear, surprise, or disgust. Use examples from past conversations if need be.

4. Ask your client about their immediate reaction or impulse to react. What did they do, or want to do, even if they didn't act on it? Discuss what the impulse was trying to seek or avoid.

5. Invite them to write or draw a symbol of the emotion on either the seeking or avoiding hand. Add what they were seeking or avoiding.

6. Repeat steps four and five with several other emotions. Invite your client to add colors, patterns, or details to show more about their experiences with seeking or avoiding.

Discussion questions:

- Do you notice more seeking or avoidant responses?

- How has seeking or avoiding helped you, even if temporarily? When has seeking or avoiding not helped? Does it ever hurt you in the long run?

- Tell me about the colors, patterns, or details you added. What do they say about your experiences of seeking and avoiding?

Helpful tip: Explore seeking or avoidant emotions that would be helpful to recruit for long-term goals. For example, if anxiety says to avoid a challenging conversation, trust might encourage seeking advice from a friend on how to approach the conversation. If anger seeks immediate resolution, empathy might suggest avoiding escalation and taking space before conversing. Add these to the hands or prompt clients to make a separate art response.

★ CAUTIOUS COMPANIONS

Clients tend to be less engaged in therapy when they feel bored, disinterested, or distracted. However, even disengaging emotions serve a valuable purpose. For starters, they are important members of the internal world that can protect clients from uncomfortable emotions and memories. They can also tell both client and therapist to proceed with caution, informing the pace of therapy. Rather than blocking progress, disengaging emotions can be recruited as trusted companions to assist in the therapeutic process.

Materials: Drawing paper (any paper works), drawing utensils (colored pencils, markers, or crayons), writing utensil

1. When your client appears sleepy, bored, disinterested, indifferent, or distracted, check in using nonjudgmental observations. Reassure them that it is okay to feel whatever they are feeling.

2. Suggest your client show what the feeling looks like, using the drawing utensils. If they say they feel "nothing," ask them to show what "nothing" looks like.

3. Provide gentle guidance as needed by offering examples like, "Would nothing be all white, all black, or a dot?"

4. Alternatively, invite your client to scrunch or rip their paper into a size and shape to represent their feeling.

5. Invite your client to look at their image or paper object and consider how this emotion may be trying to help. Ask what information or needs it might express if it could talk.

6. Invite your client to give their emotion a voice by completing the following writing prompts from the perspective of their image: "I am..."; "I wonder..."; "I pretend..."; "I worry..."; "I understand..."; "I am..." For example: "I am nothing. I wonder nothing. I pretend not to care. I worry I am failing at everything. I understand nothing. I am fed up."

Discussion questions:

- What did you learn about this feeling through your image and writing?

- What is it like to think of this feeling as trying to help? How might it be able to help you more effectively?

- If your feeling was a friend, how might you respond to it?

Helpful tip: It's okay to draw or write on behalf of your client if they are unwilling or unable to draw or write. Prompt your client to make simple choices by asking questions like, "Would it be big or small? Curvy or jagged?" Draw what they describe.

Chapter 4

SOOTHE ANGER

Soothing anger is a therapeutic priority, especially when anger is quick and intense. Yet anger reduction strategies are just as helpful for those who repress anger. When clients learn they are capable of calming their own anger, they gain confidence that encountering this emotion can be both safe and beneficial to them. Both anger-intense and anger-averse clients can also learn that soothing anger need not be an internal power struggle. Rather than trying to manage, control, or overcome anger, clients can learn to approach anger reduction as a kind and collaborative process between themselves and their emotion.

This chapter offers 10 creative approaches for soothing anger. Some activities offer artistic twists on traditional relaxation, thought replacement, and problem-solving techniques. Others use creative strategies to directly transform images of anger into soothing colors or forms. Helpful tips will guide you in adapting activities to various client needs as well as daily life, so clients can access soothing strategies outside therapy.

★ PEACEFUL PARTNERSHIP

How we talk about goals matters. While controlling, managing, or letting go of anger may all equate to reducing anger's intensity, different frameworks have different implications that can impact clients' feelings about themselves and their relationship with anger. This activity encourages clients to adopt a framework that emphasizes a peaceful partnership by *soothing anger*. It encourages intrapersonal connection and compassion, reduces internal power struggles, and supports a kind approach that can also be applied to life's challenges and relationships.

Materials: Drawing paper (any paper works), drawing utensils (colored pencils, markers, or crayons), writing utensil

1. Share common frameworks of working with anger, such as controlling, managing, overcoming, calming, and letting go.

2. Discuss your client's own past experiences of working with anger and the messages they received about how to deal with anger.

3. Fold a piece of paper into three.

4. Ask your client to label the first two sections with a different framework for working with anger. These might be frameworks they have come across in the past, such as "controlling" and "managing." Ask them to label the third section "soothing."

5. Invite your client to represent each of the three frameworks by using colors, lines, shapes, patterns, or images. Visual responses can be abstract, metaphoric, or other.

6. Support your client through each section as needed. For example, ask what "controlling" feels like, what the word reminds them of, and about its benefits and drawbacks.

Discussion questions:

- Describe your three images. What similarities and differences stand out?

- Which of these three frameworks are you most drawn to, and why?

- Which of the three frameworks do you think would benefit you most? Which would have the least or most drawbacks?

Helpful tip: Clients are not "wrong" if they decide "controlling" or "managing" anger is their preferred framework. Examine how their chosen framework serves them. Explore how and when soothing anger could become a component of their chosen framework.

★ SOLUTION SYNTHESIZER

Anger tends to decrease when we identify the anger-inducing problem and take rational steps to resolve it. However, putting a logical plan into action is not easy. Even when viable solutions are outlined in therapy, emotions and impulses run higher back in the real world. This can thwart clients' best intentions to implement solutions. Clients need more than practical steps. This activity focuses on building client confidence in their resources and abilities while giving them an enticing glimpse at relief-filled resolution.

Materials: Three pieces of drawing paper (any paper works), drawing utensils (colored pencils, markers, or crayons)

1. Invite your client to brainstorm internal and external resources that are both accessible and valuable to them. Give examples, such as friends, family, community supports, positive personality traits, and personal skills.

2. Prompt your client to create an image including some or several of their internal and external resources. Your client may create a cohesive, imaginary scene or doodle their different resources around the page.

3. On a second piece of paper, ask your client to draw an anger-related problem. It might be a problem that angers them or a problem that resulted from an angry encounter.

4. On the third piece of paper, prompt your client to create a new drawing that synthesizes their two previous images, integrating elements from both their internal and external resources and the anger-related problem image.

5. Reassure your client that it is okay if the final image does not appear to make sense. It can be nonsensical, fanciful, or literal.

6. Together, examine the final, integrated image. Discuss how the integrated image might inform a practical plan of action.

Discussion questions:

- Let's line up your images. What do you notice? Describe the feelings you get when looking at each.

- How did you decide on which elements to combine in the final image? Tell me a story about the final image.

- How might your final image inform practical steps you can take in real life to address the problem? How does the feeling you get from this image support you taking next steps to resolve this problem?

Helpful tip: Readily available images from magazines or online can provide creative inspiration as well as additional structure. If making a collage, instruct clients to create a pile of resource-related images and a pile of problem-related images. Finally, prompt them to combine the two piles into a cohesive image that they glue onto one piece of paper.

★ NEUTRALIZING COLORS

Adding a chemical base to an acid creates a unique, neutralized solution. Similarly, we can soothe anger by carefully combining it with a counteracting emotion. Different from ignoring anger or masking it with a pleasing feeling, this activity gently acknowledges anger while gradually introducing an alternative experience. In this way, clients learn to directly soothe anger while watching it transform it into something new.

Materials: Drawing paper (any paper works), drawing utensils (colored pencils, markers, or crayons)

1. Invite your client to select one color that represents anger and another that represents an anger-neutralizing color. This might be a calming or pleasant color. Remind your client that there is no right or wrong answer.

2. Explain that your client will alternate coloring with each color from opposite sides of their paper, leaving about two to three inches blank in the middle.

3. Prompt your client to begin coloring from one edge of the paper with their anger color, moving toward the middle. They can use shading, cross-hatching, scribbling, or another technique.

4. Prompt your client to switch colors, starting from the opposite side of their paper with their calming or pleasant color, and moving gradually toward the middle.

5. Invite your client to continue switching back and forth on their own, coloring with anger, then coloring with calm, and back again. The center gap will narrow.

6. Once there are two to three inches of center space left, invite your client to pause. Prompt them to consider how they will bring the two colors together to create something new. Provide creative options, such as using an entirely new color, overlapping colors, drawing swirls, or drawing a new pattern or image.

Discussion questions:

- Tell me about the colors you chose. Do they have any personal meaning or associations for you?

- What was it like to switch back and forth between the two colors? Do you think it would have felt any differently completing one color and then the other?

- What was it like to create the middle section? Does anger feel neutralized or not?

Helpful tip: Make this activity accessible anywhere. Guide your client to visualize an angry color and a neutralizing color moving toward each other. Prompt them to use their imagination to watch the transformation in the space where the two colors meet.

★ REIMAGINED ANGER

If you imagine a threat, the mind and body activate as if it were real (Reddan, Wager, and Schiller 2018). If you picture petting a beloved animal or spending quality time with a friend, the body relaxes. Because physiology responds to imagination, we can capitalize on creativity to influence not only clients' emotional states, but their physical states as well. In this activity, clients will recall comforting experiences to inspire imaginative ways to alter anger's appearance, and thus change how their mind and body responds to its presence.

Materials: Drawing paper (any paper works), drawing utensils (colored pencils, markers, or crayons)

1. Invite your client to draw any representation of anger. They may use emojis, lines, shapes, colors, forms, images, or patterns. Set this aside or turn the paper over.

2. Now invite your client to recall an experience with giving or receiving comfort, such as stroking a cat, rocking a baby, receiving a hug from a friend, or thinking good wishes for a community in need. The situation can be real or imaginary.

3. Guide your client to bring the comforting image to mind, amplifying details, colors, sounds, sensations, and feelings.

4. Ask your client to notice what happens in their mind and body. Invite them to describe sensations, feelings, and words that arise when focused on the comforting image.

5. Explain that your client will use these comforting sensations, feelings, and words to transform their original drawing of anger.

6. Invite your client to return to their original drawing to add soothing changes or additions. Offer suggestions, such as adding new patterns, shapes, or details, coloring over or around anger, or filling the rest of the page with soothing colors, images, or words.

Discussion questions:

- What was it like to draw the original representation of anger? What was it like to transform it? How do you feel when looking at your new image of anger?

- How might memories of comforting experiences soothe anger in everyday situations?

- What part of your final image is the most comforting or pleasant to you? Is there a gesture or movement that would go with that?

Helpful tip: Help your client practice this activity entirely in their imagination so they can easily use it in other settings. Guide your client to visualize what anger would look like if it had a color, shape, texture, or form. Then ask them to imagine bringing in comforting elements, such as soothing colors, or metamorphosing into a new shape or form.

★ OF MANY MINDS

Our minds have many different modes that inform how we think about and approach the world, such as work mode, play mode, angry mode, compassionate mode, emotional mode, and logical mode. Sometimes keeping modes separate is useful, like when we choose to be fully present in family mode rather than trying to mix family and work modes. But at other times it is beneficial to integrate opposing mind modes, such as when emotion and logic together provide more wisdom than operating from one mode alone. In this activity, clients will visually combine anger with another, contrasting mode to illuminate a more balanced approach to feeling, thought, and action.

Materials: Drawing paper (any paper works), drawing utensils (colored pencils, markers, or crayons)

1. Explain that our mind has different modes. For example, in angry mode we might be driven by emotion, our thoughts may be judgmental or accusatory, and we might act more abruptly, impulsively, or retaliatorily.

2. Discuss modes that could be considered opposite to angry mode, such as logical mode, compassionate mode, or problem-solving mode. Ask your client to select one that would be most helpful in times of anger.

3. Help your client draw a Venn diagram including two large, over-lapping circles.

4. In one of the circles, ask your client to use colors, lines, patterns, symbols, or words to represent their angry mode. Instruct your client to leave the overlapping portion blank.

5. In the other circle, ask your client to use colors, lines, patterns, symbols, or words to represent the opposite mode they chose. Instruct your client to leave the overlapping portion blank.

6. Discuss how working from either mode alone may pose problems.

Integrating them can lead to a balanced perspective that honors the wisdom of both modes. Invite your client to complete the overlapping portion by using new colors, lines, patterns, symbols, or words to represent an integration of the two modes.

Discussion questions:

- Describe how you represented each mode. What stands out to you?

- Which mode was easier or more difficult to create? How easy or difficult was it to combine the two modes in the center?

- What feeling do you get when you look at each mode in isolation? How does your feeling change when you look at the central, integrated mode?

Helpful tip: Simplify this activity by limiting modes to emotional mode and logical mode. Invite your client to follow the same steps, creating an integrated mode in the center that combines the wisdom of emotion and logic.

★ (UN)MASKED PORTRAIT

Calming anger too quickly can lead to unanticipated consequences. Even when clients are consciously motivated to soothe anger, their mind and body may instinctively react by strengthening defenses, shutting down, or urging risky behavior. After all, if anger is shielding them from threats or vulnerable emotions, feeling calm may unexpectedly feel unsafe. Paradoxically, sometimes soothing anger means allowing anger to remain in place. This activity helps clients keep anger safely intact while slowly nudging it aside to acknowledge feelings beneath.

Materials: Drawing paper (any paper works), pencil, drawing utensils (colored pencils, markers, or crayons)

1. Explain that your client is going to draw a portrait showing two parts of their experience: with and without anger. Offer the metaphor of a mask that covers some, or most, of the face.

2. Invite your client to draw a large outline of a head. It can be an oval. Assist if needed.

3. Invite your client to use a pencil to lightly draw a line separating the part of the portrait that will show "with anger" and the part that will represent "without anger." Encourage your client to consider how much space "with anger" will take up. It does not need to be equal.

4. Bring your client's attention to the "anger" part of the portrait. Direct your client to add features, colors, patterns, images, or words about feeling anger. It may be literal, abstract, or both.

5. Direct your client's attention to the remaining section. Ask them to add features, colors, patterns, images, or words to represent what it would be like "without anger." Remind your client that being without anger may evoke a combination of pleasant, uncomfortable, vulnerable, and relieving feelings.

6. Invite your client to consider the line between "with" and "without" anger. Ask if they would like the separation to be solid, hazy, or something else. Optionally prompt them to optionally add embellishments or marks to the line of separation.

Discussion questions:

- Which part takes up more space, "with" or "without" anger? What might the significance of that be, if any?

- Describe the space where the two parts meet. What do you notice there?

- Let's cover up each part, one at a time. What is it like looking at each part in isolation? What is it like looking at them together, as a whole?

Helpful tip: Discuss different environments, situations, or people around whom it is useful to have more coverage by anger. Discuss times it feels safer to have less coverage by anger. Invite your client to add images around their portrait to represent emotionally, physically, and relationally safe environments. Ask how these additions might change their portrait.

★ TORN TRIGGERS

Anger increases energy in preparation to fight or flee from threat. At low levels of activation, cognitive strategies for soothing anger, such as changing thought patterns or creating an action plan, may still be available. However, at heightened levels, cognitive capacities decrease and thought-based strategies may become ineffective. Even body-based relaxation strategies like deep breathing or muscle relaxation may be impractical when the body is urging the person to mobilize. At times like these, clients benefit from directing energy into active tasks instead. This activity soothes anger by first providing a safe, active outlet for anger-induced energy before transitioning clients to a slower, thoughtful pace.

Materials: Drawing paper (any paper works), pencil or pen, colored construction paper, glue stick

1. When your client shows signs of increased anger-induced energy, invite them to write down a few words to describe what is angering them. They may write it large or small.

2. Prompt your client to tear the words from their paper, and then rip the words into small pieces. Ask your client to set the scraps aside.

3. Invite your client to write more words to describe what is angering them. They might add triggers to anger from the past or what they anticipate will anger them in the future.

4. Prompt your client to tear the words from their paper and rip them into small pieces. Encourage your client to experiment with fast, slow, big, and small rips, noting different sensations and preferences. Ask your client to set the scraps aside.

5. Repeat this process until your client says they are finished, or you observe a visible decrease in energy.

6. Invite your client to select one piece of colored construction

paper onto which they will arrange and glue the torn pieces of paper into an abstract pattern.

Discussion questions:

- What was it like to write down and tear up the things that anger you?

- In what ways did your energy change during this activity? How did you feel before, during, and after?

- What was it like to create a collage out of the torn paper? What thoughts or feelings come to mind when you look at your collage now?

Helpful tip: Energetic expression can resolve anger-induced energy, but it can also momentarily spike it. If your client has a surge of energy that requires more containment, prompt them to fold their paper several times to create more resistance during ripping, direct them to slow their ripping, or provide a containing place to put scraps such as an envelope or on top of a designated sticky note.

★ RELEASE AND RELAX

Progressive relaxation, the systematic tensing and relaxing of muscle groups, teaches clients to distinguish between relaxed and tense states so they can catch early signs of anger. It also creates a bottom-up feedback loop that soothes angry emotions and thoughts by relaxing tension in the body. This activity offers a creative twist on this traditional technique, soothing anger through the benefits of progressive relaxation as well as the power of the imagination to transform our bodies and minds.

Materials: Drawing paper (any paper works), pencil, drawing utensils (colored pencils, markers, or crayons)

1. Instruct your client to tightly clench their non-dominant hand into a fist. Ask them to imagine anger clenched within their hand by visualizing a color, light, or object within.

2. Prompt your client to use their dominant hand to trace the outline of their clenched fist.

3. Instruct your client to release their clenched fist into a relaxed position on their paper, imagining the angry color, light, or object being released. Invite your client to imagine if any new color, light, or object replaces it, or not.

4. Prompt your client to use their dominant hand to trace the outline of their relaxed hand.

5. Ask your client to repeat steps one through four twice more, positioning and tracing their hand on the same paper. It is okay for tracings to overlap.

6. Invite your client to add colors, patterns, or words to their final image, taking inspiration from the colors, light, or objects they imagined.

Discussion questions:

- What did you notice when you clenched and relaxed your hand? Was it easier to trace your clenched or relaxed hand?

- Tell me about the colors, light, or objects you imagined clenching and releasing. Did your imagery stay the same or change?

- Let's look at your final image together. What do you notice? What might it tell you about your experience with holding onto or releasing anger?

Helpful tip: Make activities applicable to everyday life. Ask, "When you anger, what is the first part of the body that changes?" Guide your client to clench and release that part of the body. As they do, prompt them to visualize a color to represent anger. Guide them to watch the color change or release when they relax. Repeat.

★ LIKEABLE LAYERS

Friendly appreciation for all emotions, including challenging ones, encourages self-kindness and understanding. Like feeling empathetic toward a hurt, growling animal, we can adopt an understanding perspective toward our own anger—that it is there for a reason and is trying to help. Rather than judging, dismissing, or becoming angry at anger, kind understanding helps us respond with soothing gestures toward ourselves, which, in turn, improves our sense of safety. This activity teaches clients to soothe anger by cultivating a kind mindset toward all parts that make up who they are, including anger.

Materials: Drawing paper (any paper works), pencil, drawing utensils (colored pencils, markers, or crayons), blank nesting doll template (print or replicate from online)

1. Provide a template with a row of three, progressively smaller, nesting doll outlines. Search online for "blank nesting doll template" to print or replicate.

2. Explain that larger nesting dolls contain smaller dolls. Similarly, we contain different parts that make up who we are. Discuss the importance of practicing appreciation for all parts of our emotional world, including anger.

3. Invite your client to label the largest with the phrase, "Grateful for everything I am."

4. Above the middle doll, prompt them to write, "Grateful for my [trait/emotion] part." Ask your client to add a personality trait or emotion they like about themself.

5. Above the smallest doll, prompt your client to write, "Grateful for my angry part."

6. Invite your client to use colors, shapes, patterns, images, or words to decorate each doll. Encourage them to silently say each phrase as they decorate each doll.

Discussion questions:

- What was it like to offer appreciation for different parts of you? What was easy or difficult about it?

- Tell me about how you decorated each doll. What might it say about each trait/emotion? What might it say about how you feel toward each trait/emotion?

- What do you not appreciate about anger? How does acknowledging what you do not like about anger help or hinder you?

Helpful tip: Reassure clients that self-compassion takes practice. It can be challenging to feel kind and appreciative toward ourselves, especially toward challenging emotions like anger. Help clients practice by including more dolls representing other easy-to-like traits.

★ THE BIG POSITIVE PICTURE

Anger limits the depth and breadth of cognitive processing, especially in relation to social decision making (Weiblen *et al.* 2021). It increases reliance on stereotypes, reduces other perspective-taking, and interferes with trust in others. When angry, we fail to see the bigger picture. When we are on the lookout for threats, we are understandably not inclined to focus on the positives like strengths, resources, and helpers. This activity soothes anger by challenging clients to look at the bigger picture, reconnect with positives in their lives, and ultimately put anger back into perspective.

Materials: Drawing paper (any paper works), pencil, drawing utensils (colored pencils, markers, or crayons)

1. Invite your client to draw a very small symbol of anger. Guide them to observe anger alone on the largely blank page.

2. Ask your client to brainstorm small, pleasant moments from their week that they feel grateful for.

3. Or prime your client in advance to spend in-between session time noting or photographing pleasant moments they are grateful for. Refer to these now.

4. Prompt your client to add words, images, symbols, shapes, or colors to represent small things they are grateful for. Draw these on the same paper as their symbol of anger.

5. Next, invite your client to brainstorm broader parts of life for which they feel grateful: health, friendships, physical abilities, spiritual connections, assets, and so forth.

6. Prompt your client to add words, images, symbols, shapes, or colors to represent these broader, gratitude-inspiring parts of life.

Discussion questions:

- While looking at this image, where does your focus go? Does it focus on one element, move around, or take in the whole picture? What stands out?

- What was it like to look at anger on the paper by itself? What is it like to look at anger after adding the positives and pleasantries?

- What will you take away from this activity that could help you soothe anger during the week?

Helpful tip: Repeating exercises in therapy increases the likelihood that clients will incorporate skills into their daily life. Make a weekly check-in routine at the start of sessions by offering a sticky note on which your client draws a small symbol of anger along with four or five things they are grateful for or inspired by.

Chapter 5

AWAKEN ANGER

Anger has surprising benefits. It alerts us to unmet needs, injustices, boundary violations, and barriers to goals. In contrast to vulnerable feelings like fear and sadness, anger can motivate us to directly address problems (Carver and Harmon-Jones 2009) and inspire optimism that we can improve our circumstances (Lerner and Keltner 2001). Awakening anger also has the potential to inject us with energy (Garfinkel *et al.* 2016). When clients feel hopeless, helpless, or unmotivated, carefully accessing anger can boost them into a more active and alert state. Once clients can mobilize, they are a step closer toward greater wellbeing.

The 10 creative activities in this chapter are particularly helpful for clients who avoid, ignore, or suppress anger. Outwardly, these clients may maintain high levels of functioning and appear "fine," or they may show signs of anxiety or depression. The activities are also relevant for clients whose anger builds up over time before bursting. These clients will benefit from deliberately accessing anger earlier so they can learn from their anger and respond to it in a controlled, intentional manner.

Before using anger-awakening activities in this chapter, familiarize yourself with the self-care activities in Chapter 1 and the soothing strategies in Chapter 4. Clients may benefit from extra containment and stabilization before, during, or after awakening anger.

★ "OKAY" UMBRELLA

We all have a part of our personality that helps us function during tough times. For some people, this part is so strong they may be entirely unaware of emotional signs that something is amiss. Some may hyper-function, getting a lot accomplished, whereas others may report they are fine while it is clear to observers that they are not. This activity teaches clients that it is okay to feel not okay, while maintaining an intact sense of general security, functioning, and optimism. It is a first step in activating anger by allowing clients to peer out from beneath their umbrella of "okay-ness" to acknowledge a shifting emotional atmosphere.

Materials: Drawing paper (any paper works), pencil, drawing utensils (colored pencils, markers, or crayons)

1. Explain that we can *know* we are ultimately okay while acknowledging times we do not *feel* okay.

2. Share the metaphor of an umbrella of "okay-ness," an overarching awareness of being okay in the world. Invite your client to draw their umbrella of "okay-ness."

3. Discuss how your client's umbrella of "okay-ness" helps them. Ask how it provides comfort and perspective.

4. Explore times your client's umbrella of "okay-ness" is all-encompassing and prevents them from being aware of stress, irritation, or other emotions. Discuss the downside of disconnecting from emotions.

5. Invite your client to add weather or other environmental elements to represent emotions they tend to avoid or ignore.

6. Prompt them to add irritation, frustration, or another variation of anger, by saying, "If irritation was part of this scene, even in a small way, where would you add that?"

Discussion questions:

- Let's talk about your umbrella. How would you describe it?

- What was it like to add weather and other environmental ele-ments to represent emotions you might avoid? Describe what you added.

- Does it seem possible to let yourself acknowledge not okay feel-ings while knowing you are generally okay? How does your image reflect that, or not?

Helpful tip: Encourage clients to consider the umbrella's shape, size, and color. Is it fully open, or partially closed? Is it fully intact, or torn? For more structure or a creative boost, provide a menu of simple drawings showing different umbrellas. Prompt your client to choose one that reflects the size and durability of their "okay-ness" umbrella.

★ INSIDE-OUT ENERGY

When anger isn't the presenting problem, anger may be the emotion that needs attention most of all. Just like an outward expression of anger may protect against feeling sad, chronic states of sadness or fatigue may mask untapped anger. This activity guides clients who are struggling with sadness, depression, or hopelessness to creatively activate agitation so they can benefit from the energetic flip-side of an internalized state.

Materials: Drawing paper (any paper works), pencil, drawing utensils (colored pencils, markers, or crayons)

1. Discuss how sadness and depression typically decrease energy whereas agitation and anger increase energy. This may feel like turning inwards (depression) versus focusing energy outwards (anger).

2. Invite your client to draw a circle in the middle of their paper to represent turning inwards.

3. Ask your client to fill the circle with lines, shapes, colors, words, or images to represent low-energy feelings, sensations, and thoughts that accompany sadness or depression.

4. Prompt your client to draw four arrows radiating out from the circle, beginning at the circle's rim, and pointing toward each of the four corners of the paper.

5. Ask your client to imagine something outside of themself that feels irritating. It can be in the past, present, future, or imagined. Prompt your client to add embellishments, shapes, colors, or patterns along the arrows to create a transitional space from turning inward to focusing energy outward.

6. Invite your client to imagine slightly amplifying agitation's energy. Around the outside of the arrows, prompt them to add new lines, shapes, colors, patterns, words, or images that show a rise in energy.

Discussion questions:

- What changed the most between the center circle and outer area of your image?

- What might your image say about the relationship between sadness and agitation in your life?

- Looking at your image, do you see ways that activating agitation could be helpful in some situations?

Helpful tip: Remember to capitalize on the drawing process to shift energy. Encourage clients to increase outward-focused energy by inviting them to make swift, outward strokes of their pencil or speedy, repetitive dots with a marker. Remind clients to notice even slight energetic changes while drawing.

★ FALSE ADVERTISING

Children receive mixed guidance in how to feel and appropriately harness anger. Caregivers and schools may inadvertently communicate that anger is not nice and is therefore punishable. Some children are taught that their anger means they are ungrateful whereas others are encouraged to be the "bigger person" by tolerating wrongdoings instead of using anger to self-advocate. This activity playfully examines misleading messages about anger, and helps clients reimagine anger's potential, with a little rebranding.

Materials: Drawing paper (any paper works), drawing utensils (colored pencils, markers, or crayons)

1. Explain that your client will imagine anger is a product for sale. They will design two imaginary advertisements, one with false or negative messages about anger, and the other with neutral or positive messages.

2. Brainstorm negative messages your client received about anger. Use fill-in-the-blank prompts, such as "Anger is..." and "Anger is not..." For example, "Anger is bad" or "Anger is not nice."

3. Bring your client's attention to subtle assumptions about anger in messages like, "You should be more grateful," "Just be positive," or "Turn the other cheek."

4. Prompt your client to design a product package with warning labels or negative messages. Offer the analogy of a public service announcement against anger.

5. Next, brainstorm ways anger could be useful. Guide your client to imagine creating a rebranding campaign for anger.

6. Prompt your client to design a new product package, adding positive, neutral, or enticing messages.

Discussion questions:

- Compare the two products and their messages. What similarities or differences stand out?

- How have negative messages about anger helped you? How have negative messages about anger hindered you?

- What was it like to design a new container for anger with a positive message? How might rebranding anger help you in your life?

Helpful tip: Try this activity with individuals, pairs, or families. Use it in pairs as a springboard to explore misleading messages that influence current relationships or messages that are passed down to children. Invite families to work on product designs together to clarify how they do and don't want anger to be viewed in their family.

★ MEANNESS EXTRACTOR

Mad feelings can prompt mean behaviors. It is not uncommon for clients to have witnessed destructive anger in others or observed unkind thoughts when feeling anger within themselves. As a result, some may reject anger altogether as a hurtful, hostile, or damaging emotion. But mad and mean do not have to go together. This activity extracts meanness from mad, so clients can reclaim the helpful, assertive energy that accompanies healthy expressions of anger.

Materials: Drawing paper (any paper works), drawing utensils (colored pencils, markers, or crayons)

1. Fold a piece of paper into three equal parts. Alternatively, provide your client with three separate pieces of paper.

2. Discuss ways mad and mean tend to mix. Ask about times your client has observed this combination of mad and mean within themself or others.

3. In the first section, invite your client to use colors, lines, shapes, symbols, words, or scribbles to show a mixture of mad and mean.

4. In the second section, invite your client to use colors, lines, shapes, symbols, words, or scribbles to extract meanness from feeling mad. Provide options, such as designing a machine to remove meanness from anger or illustrating meanness inside its own container.

5. In the final section, invite your client to use colors, lines, shapes, symbols, words, or scribbles to show what mad might look like without mean. Provide options, such as drawing symbols, shapes, or other illustrations of energy, assertiveness, agency, justice, or determination.

Discussion questions:

- What was it like to separate mean and mad from one another? What did you find easy or difficult about separating them?

- Looking at your final image of mad (without mean), does it seem possible to feel mad in a way that is safe, informative, or helpful?

- What are some practical ways to use or express anger in real life without being mean?

Helpful tip: This activity separates mean from mad to increase client comfort with activating anger. However, you can adapt it to help clients who regularly express anger in hurtful ways, too. Explain that this activity is a step toward maximizing anger's benefits without the usual harmful consequences.

★ ANGERED EMPATHY

Even when anger is warranted in personal circumstances, clients may minimize hurt or unconsciously suppress anger as a self-protective strategy. Yet the same person who is unaffected by their own anger-worthy misfortunes may readily defend others facing similar injustices. This activity uses empathy to safely activate anger with the emotional distance afforded by first focusing on others.

Materials: Drawing paper (any paper works), drawing utensils (colored pencils, markers, or crayons)

1. Invite your client to recall a time they felt protective toward someone else, whether a person, animal, or group. It can be someone from the past or present, an imaginary person or animal, or a character from a story or movie.

2. Guide your client to imagine how that person, animal, or character must have felt in the situation.

3. Invite your client to use colors, lines, shapes, symbols, or images to illustrate emotions they imagine the impacted person, animal, or character felt.

4. Guide your client to next focus on the unfairness of the situation, noticing any protective or angry urges.

5. Invite your client to create a protective barrier around the person, animal, or character's emotions using colors, lines, shapes, symbols, or images.

6. Ask your client what they would ideally say to support or stand up for the person, animal, or character in this situation, such as "You don't deserve this" or "It's not your fault." Suggest adding these words.

Discussion questions:

- ◎ Describe your drawing. What feelings do you get when looking at your drawing?

- ◎ What might someone else feel when looking at this image? What might someone else feel about anyone in a similar situation?

- ◎ What tone of voice would go with the words you added? (Model different tones and styles of assertively or lovingly saying phrases.)

Helpful tip: Assess when your client is ready to consider that they, too, may be entitled to feel anger about their own circumstances. First, wonder aloud if any person in an unjust situation might be entitled to feel angry or protective. Next, wonder aloud if it is possible that others would feel empathy for your client and their situation, like your client feels empathy for others.

★ INTENSIFIED IRRITATION

Anger-intense clients must practice restraint when expressing anger. However, anger-averse clients benefit from learning to let loose. Art has long been a sanctioned arena for people to express that which they cannot in everyday life, to stretch themselves, and to challenge societal constraints. In this activity, clients will gradually expand their expressive limits, release emotional self-restraints, and intensify irritation's energy.

Materials: Drawing paper (any paper works), pencil, black marker

1. Explain the importance of tolerating, and at times increasing, irritable energy. Irritable energy can help us set boundaries and advocate for ourselves or for others.

2. Prompt your client to draw, with a black marker, a small, thick, rectangular frame in the center of their paper. Explain that this will contain their irritation.

3. Ask your client to think of something irritating, annoying, or agitating. It can be recent or in the past, a one-time incident, or a recurring situation.

4. Prompt your client to feel even the smallest amount of irritation when thinking about the situation. Then direct your client to scribble their irritation inside the small frame using a pencil.

5. Invite your client to pause and draw a larger frame around the first, creating more scribble space. Prompt your client to resume scribbling their irritation, expanding and intensifying their movements out into the new frame.

6. Repeat steps four and five, prompting your client to continue alternating between amplifying irritation (scribbling) and containing it (adding a frame). Stop when your client cannot expand their frame any further.

Discussion questions:

- What was it like to put more (or less) energy into your scribble?

- What was it like to give yourself more space to explore and express your irritable energy?

- How did you feel before, during, and after this activity?

Helpful tip: Pausing to draw frames can be a welcome form of self-containment. However, it may disrupt other clients' flow. Offer the choice to begin with three frames of increasing size, one inside the other. Prompt your client to start their scribble within the smallest frame. After 10 to 15 seconds prompt them to expand to the next frame.

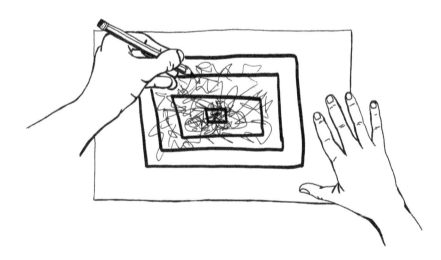

★ NOTEWORTHY NOISES

Some clients insist that they are not bothered by anything, ever, in the slightest. Those who believe positivity is the only route to wellbeing may not allow themselves to connect with words like anger, irritation, or agitation. They may even resist identifying simple symbolic shapes or colors to express anger. In this activity, clients are invited to use familiar vocalizations like "ugh" and "argh" as an initial expressive outlet for moments of displeasure.

Materials: Drawing paper (any paper works), drawing utensils (colored pencils, markers, or crayons)

1. During an initial check-in, ask your client to choose one pleasant and one undesirable situation from this past week.

2. Ask what kind of sound would go with the pleasant experience: "Was this an 'ah,' 'oh,' or 'phew' situation?" Give examples of other vocal expressions, or encourage your client to make up their own.

3. Invite your client to repeat the chosen sound with you, two to three times, lengthening the sound and exaggerating the emotion behind it.

4. Next, ask what kind of sound would go with the undesirable situation: "Was this a 'grrrrr,' 'argh,' or 'ugh' situation?" Give examples of other vocal expressions or encourage your client to make up their own.

5. Invite your client to repeat the chosen sound with you, two to three times, lengthening the sound and exaggerating the emotion behind it.

6. Suggest your client translate both sounds into a visual form using colors, lines, shapes, or patterns.

Discussion questions:

- What was it like to make each sound? What might these sounds say about emotions you had in these situations?

- Tell me about your drawings. How do the drawings express each sound differently or similarly?

- In addition to helping us acknowledge feelings, audible sighs, groans, and hums can stimulate a relaxation response (Balban *et al.* 2023; Ghati *et al.* 2021; Trivedi *et al.* 2023). Let's choose a sound to repeat together. What did you notice?

Helpful tip: Note that some sounds are easily sexualized, and certain populations will more readily make this association than others. Know your audience and use your clinical skills to accept and redirect intentional sexualization. For example, point out that while they may find the sound entertaining, it is unlikely to be an accurate match to the scenario they described.

★ PERMISSION GRANTED

Anger helps us assert boundaries, advocate for needs, and release self-blame for others' wrongdoings. But if someone believes they are not deserving of boundaries, goals, or fair treatment, it follows that anger is pointless. Once needs are reclaimed, anger has a reason to exist. This activity provides a foundational step in activating anger by reconnecting clients with basic rights to fair treatment, safety, and goals.

Materials: Scratch paper, note card (or paper cut into postcard size), drawing utensils (colored pencils, markers, or crayons)

1. Together, brainstorm general, basic human rights as well as rights specifically related to your client's unique circumstances, such as a right to "ask questions," "body boundaries," "honesty," or "understanding."

2. Invite your client to jot down rights on scratch paper. Offer to write for clients who cannot or who prefer not to write.

3. Ask your client to review the list and circle those that stand out to them as particularly helpful, important, or meaningful.

4. Invite your client to write, symbolize, or illustrate one or more of their circled rights on a note card. Prompt them to add meaningful details and embellishments.

5. Prompt your client to add one or more of these affirming phrases: "I'm allowed..."; "I deserve..."; "I give myself permission to..."; or "I have the right to..."

6. Invite your client to write a brief, encouraging message to themself on the back that reflects the theme of the front image.

Discussion questions:

- What basic rights were the easiest to connect with? Are there any rights that you think do not apply to you?

- What stands out most to you about the words and images on your note card?

- What is it like to read your message to yourself? When might your message be especially helpful in real life?

Helpful tip: If clients are not ready to fully embrace basic rights, include the phrase "I am learning…" For example, "I am learning that I'm allowed to say no" or "I am learning I have the right to ask questions." For many this feels more accurate, and makes it easier for clients to believe and affirm.

★ ANTI-ANGER AFFIRMATION

As beneficial as anger can be, it comes with many potential downsides, such as rumination, distractibility, increased blood pressure, outbursts, and disconnection. It makes sense to not want to feel angry. This activity encourages clients to brainstorm the many valid reasons for side-stepping anger. By first acknowledging what they wish to reject, clients can gain clarity about the conditions under which they would be willing to accept anger's influence.

Materials: Drawing paper (any paper works), drawing utensils (colored pencils, markers, or crayons)

1. Explain that when we know what we will not tolerate, it is easier to identify what is acceptable. For example, it is unacceptable to run near a pool; it is acceptable to walk instead.

2. Invite your client to fold a piece of paper in half. Ask your client to write, "You may not" (or "no") on one half and "You may" (or "yes") on the other half.

3. On the "You may not" side, invite your client to write what they will not tolerate from anger. For example, "You may not: keep me awake at night, make me lose my cool, or ruin my day."

4. On the "You may" side, invite your client to brainstorm what they are willing to accept from anger. For example, "You may help me be more direct, alert me to injustices, and advocate for myself and others."

5. Prompt your client to use their two brainstorms to inspire an illustration of anger with two halves, the "You may not" side representing downsides and the "You may" side representing upsides.

6. Invite your client to use the center-dividing fold as the separating line for their character or other type of illustration.

Discussion questions:

- What energy, emotions, or sensations do you feel inside when you read "You may not" phrases? What happens when you read "You may" phrases?

- Describe the two halves of your image. What do you notice about anger's downsides? What do you notice about anger's upsides?

- Do you have any new or different impressions of anger after doing this activity, or not?

Helpful tip: Young clients or literal thinkers may need to focus on observable anger-driven behaviors, such as "Anger, you may not make me hit others. You may help me use my strong voice instead." When used in this way, this activity can also help with redirecting anger toward preferred behaviors (turn to Chapter 6 for more ways to harness anger).

★ SOWING SEEDS OF ANGER

Like a seed, people have everything they need inside of themselves to grow, if environmental conditions are right. With empathy and respect for a client's current state and pace, their emotional range and ability to rebound from discomfort can flourish. Growth cannot be rushed, and nor should activating anger. This activity invites clients to plant their own seed of anger, including everything it has inside and everything it needs outside to eventually grow into healthy self-empowerment.

Materials: Drawing paper (any paper works), drawing utensils (colored pencils, markers, or crayons)

1. Invite your client to imagine they have a seed of anger that can grow into healthy empowerment.

2. Prompt your client to draw a large seed shape on their paper.

3. Invite your client to imagine using a microscope to reveal the internal parts of their anger (or empowerment) seed.

4. Encourage your client to add colors, lines, shapes, words, or symbols to show what makes up the parts of their seed.

5. Invite your client to consider the environmental conditions needed for their seed to grow. Prompt your client to use colors, lines, shapes, words, or symbols to add desirable environmental conditions.

6. Optionally, invite your client to add an illustration of what they hope their seed will eventually grow into. They may do this in the corner, on the back, or on a separate piece of paper.

Discussion questions:

- Describe your seed. What are the most essential components?

- What do you notice about the seed's environment? Describe how it will help the seed grow.

- Are there any internal or environmental factors that would prevent the seed's growth?

Helpful tip: Clients may need help brainstorming meaningful "seed anatomy," such as memories, personality traits, inspiration from role models, and values. Provide more structure if needed by dividing the seed into three parts, such as (1) plant parts representing self-empowerment potential; (2) nutrients representing energy and values; and (3) a protective casing representing self-care.

Chapter 6

HARNESS ANGER

In previous chapters, we developed self-care practices, got to know anger, and recruited other emotions. We also used art to soothe and activate angry energy, continually seeking the sweet spot between containment and expression. Building on these skills, we now use creativity to harness anger, directing its helpful potential toward desirable goals, such as setting boundaries, asking for help, and resolving past hurts. Harnessing anger not only helps clients make positive life changes; it also brings anger to resolution by allowing its purpose to be served.

This chapter contains 10 creative activities to harness anger toward beneficial outcomes. You will find activities to help clients use their anger to pursue justice, grieve past injuries, and eliminate self-blame. You will also find activities that more generally examine anger's role in motivation and living in alignment with values. As anger turns into directed action, continue monitoring and adjusting the balance between activation and soothing to optimize successful outcomes.

★ MOTIVATED MINDSET

People are motivated by many things: rewards, acknowledgments, values, social connections, avoidance of negative consequences, and even anger. Anger is energizing, but that energy can lack direction or easily become misdirected. Although angry energy is commonly recognized for providing an athletic competitive edge, it is not often acknowledged as a useful, invigorating advantage in other parts of life. This activity challenges assumptions that anger is a reactive impulse and reframes it as motivation for a proactive, motivated mindset.

Materials: Two pieces of drawing paper (any paper works), drawing utensils (colored pencils, markers, or crayons)

1. Ask your client to describe an experience in which they felt either stifled or impulsive because of angry feelings.

2. Invite your client to use colors, lines, shapes, patterns, or symbols to show how angry energy feels when it is stifled, directionless, or misdirected.

3. Divide a second piece of paper into four sections. Outline key components of motivation including focusing on a goal, energizing, starting, and persisting. Label each section: "focus," "energize," "start," and "keep going."

4. Explain that your client will now reimagine anger's energy as helpful in each stage of motivation. Start with "focus." Help your client identify an underlying, desired goal related to the previously discussed situation. Or they can pick a new situation. Prompt your client to use colors, lines, shapes, patterns, or images to show how anger helps them to clarify and focus on the goal. Their image may be abstract or literal.

5. Invite your client to fill in the remaining three sections in order, using colors, lines, shapes, patterns, or images to show anger's motivating or energizing role in each.

Discussion questions:

- Compare your image of directionless anger with your images of anger at each stage of motivation. What do you notice?

- What stands out to you about anger's role in motivation? At which stage might anger help most: "focus," "energize," "start," or "keep going?"

- How might thinking about anger as motivation help you during this upcoming week?

Helpful tip: Consider focusing on one phase of motivation per session, rather than completing all four of them in a single sitting. This will simplify the activity for younger individuals or those who overwhelm easily. For others, focusing on a single phase of motivation at a time may invite more depth of exploration.

★ REWARDS WITHIN REACH

Because anger is often a response to a threat, it follows that anger would increase our attention to other dangers. However, surprising research has shown that this is not always the case. In one study, while anxiety increased a focus on threats, anger increased attention to rewards (Ford *et al.* 2010). It has also been shown that when rewards are obtainable, anger motivates us to go after them (Aarts *et al.* 2010). This activity capitalizes on anger's drive to go after goodies by helping clients imagine how anger can help them achieve identifiable rewards within reach.

Materials: Drawing paper (any paper works), drawing utensils (colored pencils, markers, or crayons)

1. Discuss rewards that anger can help us obtain, such as protection, fair treatment, boundaries, creativity, and athletic achievement. Brainstorm specific benefits within these that are relevant to your client, such as a pay raise, personal space, or help with homework.

2. Invite your client to illustrate anger in the center of their paper as a character, emoji, or abstract form using colors, lines, or shapes. Substitute the word "assertive," or another relevant word, instead of "anger," if helpful.

3. Prompt your client to draw three block arrows pointing outward from the center image.

4. Ask your client what positive rewards the anger character would like to help them achieve. Rewards may be easily achievable or require persistence.

5. Invite your client to write or draw a symbol of a reward at the end of each arrow.

6. Invite your client to decorate the arrows with colors, patterns, or words to illustrate anger's transformation into inspiration or action. Drawings may be abstract or include specific actions your client will take toward their goals.

Discussion questions:

- Which of these goals seems easiest to achieve? Which will be most difficult?

- Tell me about your image of anger in the center and how it transforms when directed toward each goal.

- How might anger (or assertiveness) specifically help you achieve each goal? What steps will you take, and how will you adjust for each different goal?

Helpful tip: Many clients benefit from breaking goals down into smaller steps. Consider using this activity to closely examine one goal instead of three. After illustrating anger in the center and drawing arrows, prompt clients to illustrate three achievable steps toward the one goal.

★ BLAME CHANGER

Traumatic situations are neither invited nor wanted, and yet survivors of trauma commonly feel angry toward themselves. Believing "it's my fault" provides a sense of control. It is as if the mind says, "If I am to blame, I can prevent bad things from happening again." But self-blame also comes with a high emotional price including general self-doubt, anxiety, and depression, to name a few examples. This activity invites clients to transform self-blame into self-empowerment by directing kindness inwards and redirecting anger outwards.

Materials: Drawing paper (any paper works), drawing utensils (colored pencils, markers, or crayons)

1. Explain why self-blame is a common response to trauma and adverse life events. Share that this activity will explore the differences between self-blame and self-empowerment.

2. Invite your client to draw three concentric rings, leaving plenty of space around the outermost ring.

3. In the center ring, invite your client to illustrate feelings, energy, or thoughts that accompany self-blame. Provide simple options like writing the word "guilt" in a representational size, color, and font.

4. Guide your client to imagine the center ring is a separate entity or friend. In the next ring, invite your client to illustrate feelings, energy, or thoughts that offer soothing kindness and compassion toward self-blame.

5. Now invite your client to consider how they would feel toward a hypothetical person who hurt someone else. Ask if they might feel anger or blame toward them. In the next ring, invite your client to illustrate these feelings, energies, or thoughts using colors, lines, shapes, words, or symbols.

6. Finally, discuss anger's role in self-empowerment to promote feelings of safety and security. In the remaining blank area

surrounding all the rings, invite your client to illustrate feelings, energies, or thoughts related to self-empowerment.

Discussion questions:

- Which sections were easiest to create? Which were challenging to create, if any?

- Looking at your image, describe how self-empowerment differs from self-blame. Are there any similarities?

- What is it like looking at the whole image? How might self-kindness and anger toward others help transition self-blame into self-empowerment?

Helpful tip: Working with trauma requires a high degree of professional skill to monitor subtle responses and adjust interventions to maximize client feelings of safety, connection, and control. Provide additional containment by facilitating just the first two images in a single session. Complete the second two images on a different day. Check in throughout, and as needed bring your client's awareness to cues of safety in the room or shift to a self-care or soothing activity from Chapters 1 or 4.

★ VENGE-LESS VALUES

Anger can help people live in alignment with important values. Anger can alert us to what is right and wrong (Lindebaum and Geddes 2015), and motivate us to stand up for what we believe in (Halmburger, Baumert, and Schmitt 2015). However, anger can also prompt judgmental thoughts and vengeful impulses that do not necessarily match our morals. This activity redirects anger away from revenge by digging deeper within to reveal the hidden gems of personal values.

Materials: Drawing paper (any paper works), drawing utensils (colored pencils, markers, or crayons)

1. Explain that this activity will redirect anger away from vengeful or judgmental thoughts toward clarifying personal values.

2. Together, brainstorm what behaviors your client finds aggravating. Discuss feelings and sensations as well as judgmental or vengeful thoughts.

3. Invite your client to draw and label rocks representing behaviors or scenarios that illicit anger. Prompt them to consider the shape, texture, and size of the rocks.

4. Help your client identify positive core values related to each annoyance. For example, if your client angers when people brag, they might value humbleness.

5. Ask your client to imagine splitting each rock to reveal hidden gems, representing core values. Invite your client to draw gems and label them with personal values related to each irritant.

6. Invite your client to draw additional gems to represent other values that could help them when aggravated.

Discussion questions:

- Which rock stands out the most? What about it stands out to you? Which gem stands out the most? What about it stands out to you?

- Which values are easiest to act in alignment with? Which values are harder to act in alignment with?

- How might using anger to clarify morals and values help you feel or respond differently in aggravating situations?

Helpful tip: Art activities can be worked in organically during a conversation. When a client talks about an angry encounter or shares vengeful thoughts, ask if it is okay to pause the conversation to dive deeper into the topic with a creative activity. They may create one representative rock with many gems, symbolizing several values hidden beneath their anger.

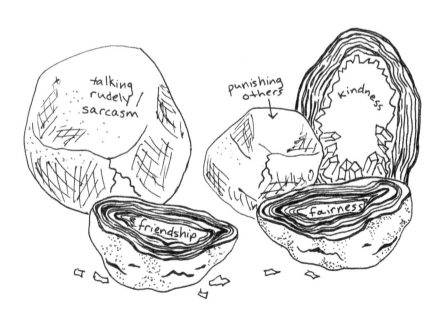

★ SPEAK-UP SUPPORTER

It is natural to avoid conflict. At times it is the safest option. Yet keeping quiet also has its downsides, including feeling disempowered, being taken advantage of, and feeling guilty for not speaking up for what you feel is right. One of anger's great gifts is its potential to help people overcome their fear of standing up for themselves and others when the time is right. Whether you use this activity to help clients heal the past by saying what was never said, or rehearse for future injustices, this activity will help clients harness anger as a super-supporter for speaking up.

Materials: Drawing paper (any paper works), drawing utensils (colored pencils, markers, or crayons)

1. Roughly draw a large outline of a person's chin, neck, shoulders, and mouth.

2. Discuss a time that your client would benefit from speaking up for themselves, a loved one, or an acquaintance. It could be in the past or future.

3. Invite your client to illustrate an imaginary barrier within the person that prevents words from coming out.

4. Prompt them to add colors or shapes to illustrate tension, constriction, or other sensations beneath or around the barrier.

5. Discuss anger's helpfulness in standing up for what's right. Ask, "What would anger say if it stood up for you?" Prompt them to illustrate anger's energy moving around, over, or through the barrier, filling the figure as much or as little as feels comfortable.

6. Invite your client to add words illustrating what anger would say on their behalf. Gently ask if they would like to write words emerging from the mouth.

Discussion questions:

- What did you notice about the barrier before and after recruiting anger as an ally?

- Would you like to read out loud what you wrote? What is it like to say these words out loud?

- What variation of these words or phrases would you use in real life, if at all?

Helpful tip: Clients gain emotional distance from the difficult task of speaking up by imagining anger doing it on their behalf. If clients would benefit from even more distance, invite them to first imagine anger standing up for a friend, animal, or child. After practicing on someone else, they may be ready to imagine anger standing up for them.

★ HELPFUL HUMOR

Finding humor in everyday misfortunes can transform maddening situations into comedic tales of human life. Different from aggressive jokes, put-downs, or sarcasm, finding the hilarity of anger-inducing rejection, mistakes, mishaps, and miscommunication eases anger and empowers us to move forward (Torres-Marín, Navarro-Carrillo, and Carretero-Dios 2018). Laughter is healing (Louie, Brook, and Frates 2016). This activity helps clients harness anger with humor by transforming the frustratingly unfair into normal, laughable parts of life.

Materials: Drawing paper (any paper works), drawing utensils (colored pencils, markers, or crayons), writing utensil, an artifact from a maddening situation, such as a rejection letter, irritating phone text, poor performance evaluation, or marked-up test

1. Clarify the difference between the helpfulness of light-hearted humor versus the harmfulness of making fun, put-downs, or passive-aggressiveness.

2. Invite your client to share an artifact of a maddening encounter such as a rejection letter, irritating phone text, poor performance evaluation, or marked-up test. If they do not have the artifact, invite them to roughly reproduce it.

3. Alternatively, invite your client to create a make-believe message based on an in-person interaction. For example, a teen who has lost privileges might create an imaginary note saying, "Grounded. Forever."

4. Offer a friendly challenge to think of ways to make the artifact comical. Brainstorm ideas for transforming the artifact, like dotting the "I's" with poop emojis, folding it into a paper airplane and decorating it, adding a funny cartoon character speaking the words, or transforming it into a valentine or party invitation.

5. Invite your client to make funny additions or changes directly to the original document or replica.

6. Encourage your client to consider what more might be comedic about the situation or the artifact. What about it is relatable to others? Optionally, invite your client to visualize or act out how a comedian would use this situation as material in a stand-up comedy show.

Discussion questions:

● How do you feel when looking at your artifact now? What new beliefs about yourself or the situation arise?

● How did adding humor impact angry feelings? What are ways you might bring humor to everyday, maddening events?

● What are ways you can use humor to help yourself without appearing uncaring or disrespectful to others?

Helpful tip: Some clients may struggle with the idea that something upsetting can also be funny. That's okay. Gently challenge the misconception that finding humor in something means it is unimportant. Or, instead of making the artifact humorous, suggest transforming it in any way that feels empowering.

★ NEAT AND NARROW

Sometimes people feel generally irritable, and they don't know why. When sources of anger are unidentified or ignored for long enough, agitation can overflow into situations and relationships unrelated to the original source of anger. Unless we identify the irritating issue and take steps to resolve it, general irritability will likely persist. This activity helps clients direct anger in a neat and narrow direction, reducing unnecessary overflow into unrelated areas of life.

Materials: Drawing paper (any paper works), drawing utensils (colored pencils, markers, or crayons)

1. Prompt your client to draw a simple bird's-eye view of a river that is wide at the bottom of the paper and narrows as it moves towards the top.

2. Explain that just like a river moves in one general direction, anger can move us toward resolving a targeted problem. However, anger can also overflow, become misdirected, or muddy the waters.

3. Invite your client to write all that has felt agitating lately on the riverbank. Encourage your client to not dismiss anything as unimportant. If relevant, include anticipated, upcoming situations.

4. Prompt your client further to illustrate anger's overflow and misdirection by adding colors, lines, shapes, or images to the riverbank.

5. Invite your client to look at their image and identify which of the irritants stands out most, either visually or emotionally.

6. Prompt your client to focus their attention and energy on this one situation while adding colors, lines, shapes, or words inside the river. Encourage experimentation with the concept of directing anger in one direction.

Discussion questions:

- What was it like to draw anger's overflow and misdirection? What do you notice when looking at that part of the drawing?

- Describe the river. How is the focus and direction of the river different from the overflow of the riverbank?

- Did anything change between the wide and narrow ends of the river, or not? How might narrowing in on what bothers you help you resolve your feelings of irritability?

Helpful tip: Consider expanding this activity by inviting clients to add stepping-stones to the river on which they can identify practical, sequential steps to resolve the situation.

★ ASSERTIVE BALANCING ACT

Anger can make us judge others more harshly and cut corners cognitively by relying on broad beliefs rather than nuanced reasoning (Lerner and Shonk 2010). Add to this increased impulsivity and the result is over-reaction. On the flip-side, those who are conflict-avoidant or who tend to shut down in maddening situations may under-respond, missing opportunities to harness anger toward meaningful change. These extremes often have long-term consequences and are likely less effective than a more balanced, assertive response. This activity helps clients harness anger toward a balance between assertiveness, confidence, and kindness, so they can uncover a broader range of choices for resolution.

Materials: Drawing paper (any paper works), drawing utensils (colored pencils, markers, or crayons)

1. Discuss times your client under-responded to a maddening situation by avoiding it, biting their tongue, or convincing themself it was "fine." Alternatively, invite your client to imagine what under-responding might feel like.

2. Ask your client to abstractly illustrate the feeling of under-responding on one side of their paper by using colors, lines, shapes, symbols, words, or patterns.

3. Next, discuss times your client may have over-responded in a maddening situation by shouting, using unkind words, throwing or slamming something, or ignoring someone for a prolonged period. If they have not had an over-responding experience, invite your client to imagine what it might feel like.

4. Ask your client to abstractly illustrate the feeling of over-responding on the other side of their paper by using colors, lines, shapes, symbols, words, or patterns.

5. Finally, discuss times your client responded to anger in a balanced

manner. Discuss elements of assertiveness, confidence, and kindness.

6. Prompt your client to abstractly illustrate a balanced response to a maddening situation in the center of their paper by using colors, lines, shapes, symbols, words, or patterns.

Discussion questions:

- Describe the emotions and sensations that come with under-reacting, over-reacting, and assertive (or balanced) responses. How did you illustrate these feelings in your drawings?

- Which response is your automatic go-to? Which do you linger in longest?

- Take a moment to focus on the middle, balanced section. What happens inside your mind and body? How might a balanced state help broaden your range of choices for resolution?

Helpful tip: If clients struggle to abstractly illustrate emotions or sensations, provide the option to draw an angry character engaged in over-responding, under-responding, and balanced behaviors. Alternatively, develop your client's ability to notice feelings and sensations accompanying states of under- and over-responding by first exploring familiar spectrums, such as "starving" (under-fed), "stuffed" (over-fed), and "content" (balanced).

★ DETERMINED CLIMB

Anger is goal-driven, so when objectives are thwarted, anger will let it be known. Yet, as determined as anger can be to help us succeed, it can just as easily get distracted. Instead of maneuvering around obstacles, anger can fixate on barriers, depleting valuable time and energy. To persevere toward long-term goals, it is important to direct anger away from preoccupations with an obstacle's existence, and toward persistence and planning to bypass barriers (Schmitt, Gielnik, and Seibel 2019). This activity prepares for both opportunities and barriers so clients can sustain the lengthy climb toward long-term goals.

Materials: Drawing paper (any paper works), drawing utensils (colored pencils, markers, or crayons)

1. Ask your client to choose a long-term goal to focus on for this activity. Or introduce this activity when your client brings up frustrations about a goal, such as getting onto a team, finding a job, or meeting a life-long partner.

2. Invite your client to draw a mountain. Explain that the summit signifies goal achievement.

3. Prompt your client to place a figure, stick person, or shape somewhere on the paper to signify where they are currently in their progress toward reaching the top.

4. Invite your client to draw elements on the mountain to represent angering obstacles they have encountered or may still face along the way. Give examples like boulders, crevasses, or fallen trees to symbolize barriers.

5. Invite your client to add elements in the mountain terrain that symbolize opportunities they have encountered or may come across along the way to their goal. Give examples like fellow hikers, shade, or climbing ropes to symbolize opportunities.

6. Prompt your client to draw paths, back-up plans, or symbolic

solutions for bypassing or directly dealing with obstacles while taking advantage of opportunities.

Discussion questions:

- In what ways does anger help or hinder your long-term goal achievement? Which obstacles are surprising? Which are predictable? Which become draining distractions?

- What is it like looking at the whole picture, including obstacles and opportunities? How might keeping the big picture in mind help direct energy toward your goal?

- What specific, achievable plans and back-up plans can you make now to deal with real-life angering obstacles?

Helpful tip: Some clients believe it is necessary to feel anger at people who impede their path in order to reach their goal. Help clients re-examine this assumption. When does going around an obstacle conserve more resources than trying to remove or push through an obstacle? Do they have what they need to get to the summit, without the other person's support?

★ CATHARTIC CREATIVITY

It is not healthy to stew in anger, yet many clients are not ready to take anger-motivated action to resolve maddening situations. Some may never want to stand up to another; others may determine it would not be safe or useful; and some may never get the opportunity, even if they want it. For others, an injustice may be so large that there is no person, per se, to stand up to. Luckily, resolving anger does not require saying (or hearing) the right thing, confronting others, or making a substantial gesture of social action. Instead, clients can harness anger toward controlled, creative release as an alternative for alleviating angry energy.

Materials: Colored pipe cleaners

1. While your client discusses a maddening situation, invite them to play and experiment with pipe cleaners.

2. Suggest your client bring their attention to how their angry energy feels inside. Prompt them to imagine infusing the pipe cleaners with that energy.

3. Invite your client to bend one, two, or many pipe cleaners into a form that represents how their anger feels when it is stuck or has nowhere to go.

4. Next, invite your client to imagine being able to move the angry energy. Prompt your client to manipulate the pipe cleaners to show how anger would change if it had movement.

5. Remind your client that they do not need to know how anger would move or what form it would take. Encourage them to spontaneously explore its flexible, creative potential. It does not need to make sense.

6. Ask, "If anger could transform into something creative, helpful, or resolved, what form would it take?" Ask if they would like to remove or add pipe cleaners, give them more or less energy and space, or transform them into a final shape.

Discussion questions:

- How do you feel now, compared to when we started? Was there any part of this activity that you particularly liked?

- Anger can increase unstructured flexible thinking (Baas, De Dreu, and Nijstad 2011). What was this process like for you? What was it like to work with a less structured, flexible material?

- Describe how the pipe cleaners changed throughout this activity. What does that say about how anger can change within you?

Helpful tip: Large, expressive, and uncontrollable cathartic release can feel scary and re-traumatizing to clients. That is why it is important to offer a creative material that is flexible, offers movement, and has transformative properties while still being structured and controllable. If clients would benefit from larger body movement that is still well regulated, attach two or three pipe cleaners together to create longer pieces for your client to manipulate.

Chapter 7

NAVIGATE ANGER IN RELATIONSHIPS

Anger is an interpersonal issue as much as it is an individual matter. Anger is often provoked within relationships, and when it isn't, anger is commonly misdirected onto loved ones. If unresolved, anger breeds resentment, hurt, and disconnection. But when addressed thoughtfully, it can enhance emotional safety, communication, and closeness. Activities throughout this book will naturally decrease anger's negative impact on relationships. After all, when we work on our own relationship with anger, personal relationships also benefit. In this chapter, however, we will specifically use creative activities to quickly illuminate relationship dynamics, diffuse relationship tension, and prompt new ways of interacting.

In this chapter you will find 10 creative activities to improve boundaries, repair ruptures, manage expectations, communicate needs, and more. Some activities focus on helping the angered individual whereas others support those who are targets of anger. You will also find helpful tips to adapt activities when working with couples, families, and parent–child dyads. Feel free to apply one activity's helpful tips to other activities. Relationships are complicated, so read the activity descriptions and use your clinical judgment to determine which activities and adaptations are most suitable to your treatment unit and goals.

★ BOUNDARY BUILDER

Anger reminds us to set limits when our physical or emotional boundaries are crossed. Yet knowing when and how firmly to enforce boundaries is not easy, especially when different situations require different responses. This activity helps clients harness anger to build healthier boundaries so they can maintain comfortable levels of connection while protecting precious resources like time, emotions, energy, material things, and space.

Materials: Drawing paper (any paper works), drawing utensils (colored pencils, markers, or crayons)

1. Ask your client to imagine a person who is easy to be around. Ask them to draw one shape to represent themself and another shape to represent the easy-to-be-around person.

2. Prompt your client to draw a boundary between the two shapes, symbolically illustrating how thick or thin, tall or short, and permeable or solid it is.

3. Invite your client to consider details like what material their boundary would be made of, or whether it has a gate or a door.

4. Next, prompt your client to add a shape that represents a challenging person. It might be someone who takes advantage of your client's time, emotions, energy, things, or personal space.

5. Invite your client to symbolically draw the boundary that exists between themself and the challenging person, considering its size, material, and other details.

6. Discuss how anger can serve a healthy, self-protective role. Ask your client to consider how anger could help them modify either or both boundaries. Prompt them to make those changes on their paper.

Discussion questions:

- Compare and contrast the boundaries you have drawn. What do you notice?

- How does anger impact your boundaries in positive or negative ways?

- Tell me about the improvements you made. How can you translate your modifications into real-world change?

Helpful tip: Some clients need help relaxing boundaries instead of strengthening them. Help clients approach boundary-setting in a nuanced way by developing different boundaries for different relationships. Guide them to imagine ways to soothe anger where boundaries are unnecessarily rigid (see Chapter 4) and activate anger where boundaries need strengthening (see Chapter 5).

★ NOT MY ANGER

We are wired to literally feel others' emotions. Empathy connects us to one another, but it can also be overwhelming when we experience our own and others' emotions concurrently. Not only does experiencing others' feelings require more emotional information processing, but it can also become difficult to distinguish our own emotions from those belonging to others. This activity helps clients disentangle others' anger from their own, so they feel less overwhelmed and are better able to pursue personally meaningful choices.

Materials: Two pieces of drawing paper (any paper works), drawing utensils (colored pencils, markers, or crayons)

1. Invite your client to select one color to represent their anger and a different color to represent another person's anger.

2. Allow your client to select as many colors as needed to represent anger belonging to other identified individuals, groups, or communities.

3. Encourage your client to create a key to show which color corresponds with each person, group, or community.

4. Prompt your client to scribble the size, shape, and intensity of their own anger using their personal color.

5. Prompt your client to use each of the other colors to scribble the size, shape, and intensity of others' anger. Encourage overlapping scribbles to illustrate how entangled the emotions are.

6. On another piece of paper, invite your client to draw and label each scribble separately, within their own space on the page. Encourage your client to illustrate any changes in size, shape, or intensity once they are disentangled from the others.

Discussion questions:

- Let's compare the two drawings. How would you describe the first and second drawings? What would you title each of these?

- Did your own anger change or stay the same from one drawing to the next? In what ways?

- How does being tangled up with others' emotions impact your decisions? Does disentangling your own anger from others' anger change the choices you might make?

Helpful tip: Invite each person in a family to complete this activity separately to reveal information about emotional dynamics. Suggest clients incorporate other emotions that, when combined, lead to anger in their relationship. For example, "Your worry tangles with my stress, which creates a ball of anger."

★ ANGER'S IMPACT

A surge of intense anger may get us what we want in the short term, but even brief blow-ups can cause lasting harm to relationships. The challenge is helping clients pause long enough in a maddening moment to see the bigger picture and take a different course of action. After all, outbursts get quick compliance, which is highly rewarding. This activity helps clients see the bigger picture by acknowledging both the relief they receive from bursts of anger as well as the relationship prices they will eventually pay.

Materials: Drawing paper (any paper works), drawing utensils (colored pencils, markers, or crayons)

1. Invite your client to select a color to represent discomfort that arises from an angering situation. Prompt them to color a small scribble or sunburst in the center of their paper illustrating feelings or sensations before their anger bursts.

2. Ask your client to select a new color representing their outward surge of anger. Prompt them to color a sunburst around the first color to illustrate the moment of the angry outburst.

3. Discuss short-term benefits that come from a burst of intense anger. For example, anger might alleviate discomfort by achieving quick compliance from others, getting you needed space, or ending an uncomfortable conversation.

4. Invite your client to select another color to draw a new ring, representing good feelings that arise after a surge of anger. They may draw another sunburst or use a different line quality.

5. Next, brainstorm short- and long-term costs of anger outbursts. Remind your client that these may be invisible or develop over time, such as feeling guilt, receiving a backlash of anger or resentment, eroding a loved one's self-esteem, or becoming disconnected.

6. Invite your client to select a new color to represent the cost of anger, using it to draw a final, illustrative ring.

Discussion questions:

- The rings remind me of throwing a stone in the water. It has an immediate impact and a long-lasting rippling effect. Anger can be like that. What does your image remind you of, if anything?

- What is it like to look at the whole picture, including early discomfort, anger, relief, and lasting impact? What stands out?

- What would you change about your image to achieve benefits while minimizing long-term consequences?

Helpful tip: Invite clients to label each ring of color with their feelings and needs at that stage. For example, "Discomfort: I feel stressed. I need cooperation so we're not late." "Anger: I feel unheard. I need people to pay attention." "Relief: I'm glad people are listening." And so forth.

★ RUPTURE REPAIR

A vital part of working with anger is relationship repair. All too often, people sweep anger-inducing incidents under the rug, either minimizing others' hurt for the sake of self-preservation or wrongly believing that "sorry" is enough. Even as clients learn to express anger in healthier ways, past relationship ruptures will likely still require attention. This activity highlights the significant impact of relationship ruptures while building foundational skills to initiate sincere repairs.

Materials: Drawing paper (any paper works), drawing utensils (colored pencils, markers, or crayons), tape

1. Explain that conflicts and misunderstandings, both big and small, can cause relationship ruptures. Discuss relationship ruptures your client has experienced, or point out a recent example your client has shared.

2. Ask your client to thoughtfully make a tear in their paper illustrating the size and significance of a relationship rupture. They can make a tiny tear that keeps the paper intact, a long tear that separates the paper, or a tear that removes a chunk. Remind your client that even small disagreements can cause large ruptures.

3. Invite your client to add lines, shapes, colors, words, or symbols on one side of the tear, illustrating their own emotions and needs related to what caused the rupture.

4. Invite your client to add lines, shapes, colors, words, or symbols on the other side of the tear, showing the other person's emotions and needs related to what caused the rupture.

5. Optionally, repeat steps two through four on the same piece of paper, calling to mind other ruptures in the same relationship. Discuss the impact of multiple tears on one piece of paper and how this might relate to the impact of multiple ruptures on a relationship.

6. Invite your client to apply as many strips of tape as they think sufficient to repair the tears. Discuss how bigger tears require more tape, just like bigger relationship ruptures require more effort to rebuild connection.

Discussion questions:

- Let's look at your piece of paper together. How did the tears impact the paper? What was it like to tape the tears back together?

- How did the size of tear inform its repair? How might your experience with this project motivate relationship repair in real life?

- Tell me about your feelings and needs, and the other person's feelings and needs. Can you see any of their feelings or needs as valid, or not? What, if anything, can you take accountability for in the rupture?

Helpful tip: Emphasize the importance of deeply acknowledging the other person's needs and feelings when making repairs. Let clients know they can practice this by describing their art response to the other person. Talking about art offers a comfortable buffer when learning to share acknowledgments and apologies with loved ones.

★ LOVE AND LIMITS

Healthy relationships require expressions of both love and limits. A parent says "I love you" and maintains rules for safety and respect. A boss shows appreciation for employees and reinforces deadlines. Siblings learn to share and ask before taking. When love and limits are balanced, relationships feel safe and supportive, but when the scales tip too far toward unhealthy permissiveness or harshness, relationships become unstable, and anger may flare. This activity helps clients identify which direction they automatically lean in, and invites them to regain balance.

Materials: Drawing paper (any paper works), drawing utensils (colored pencils, markers, or crayons)

1. Discuss the importance of finding a balance between expressing love and enforcing limits in relationships.

2. Ask your client which mode they lean more heavily on—expressions of caring and nurturance or enforcement of expectations and limits.

3. Invite your client to use colors, lines, shapes, words, or symbols to illustrate how they feel when operating from their primary mode.

4. Next, ask your client to illustrate how they feel (or can imagine feeling) when operating from their non-primary mode.

5. Invite your client to reflect on how and when anger arises in their relationships because of an imbalance between care and limits. Prompt them to illustrate this using colors, lines, shapes, words, or symbols.

6. Optionally, invite your client to make changes to their final image to improve the balance between expressions of care and limits.

Discussion questions:

- What stands out to you in your image?

- Tell me about anger's role in this image. Is there a story behind it?

- How might a greater balance of love and limits change your own feelings? How might a greater balance of love and limits impact your relationship?

Helpful tip: If clients struggle to draw feelings, invite them to make two separate lists, one describing words and actions they use to communicate care, and another with words and actions they use to enforce limits. Ask them to draw a different shape around each list, fitting that list's theme. Finally, invite them to adjust their lists to create balance and draw a bridge between the shapes.

★ CRISSCROSSED COMMUNICATION

Poor communication is a common root of anger. Two people, desperate to be understood, validated, and supported, bounce remarks off each other, without their messages ever landing on attentive, empathic ears. Both people need to be heard. Neither truly listen. Anger sparks. This activity helps pairs work together to slow communication down, take turns, and replace crisscrossed communication with connection.

Materials: Drawing paper (any paper works), drawing utensils (colored pencils, markers, or crayons)

1. Prompt each client to select one drawing utensil.

2. Invite your clients to imagine a crisscross pattern that incorporates both colors.

3. Instruct your clients to focus on their own imagined pattern without communicating it verbally to their partner. Prompt them to simultaneously draw their crisscrossed pattern, each with their own color, on the same piece of paper.

4. Observe their process. Discuss what happened when they focused on their own desired outcome. What worked, and what did not? What was easy or difficult?

5. Now, task your clients with collaborating on a pattern that represents "connection," using both colors. Let them know they can discuss ideas.

6. Observe their process. Discuss what happened when they collaborated. What worked and what did not? What was easy or difficult?

Discussion questions:

- What comes to mind when you think of crisscrossed communication? What comes to mind when you think of connected communication?

- What stands out when looking at the patterns? Which was easier to make? Which did you enjoy making more?

- How did interactions during this activity reflect your typical communication patterns? What interactions were new or different?

Helpful tip: Thoughtfully consider how much you will observe and how much you will intervene during the activity. You can watch interactions to gather information about communication patterns, intervening only to support emotional safety if frustrations rise. Or you can actively intervene to prompt clients to take turns, listen, reflect on what was heard, and make requests during the activity.

★ BEFORE THE FINAL STRAW

Relationships can flourish when we give each other the benefit of the doubt and let some things go. Not every slight miscommunication or mismatched need requires a conversation. However, many minor missteps may amount to a hefty sense of wrongdoing over time. When we let too many ruptures go unaddressed, anger can seemingly appear out of nowhere. This activity helps clients learn when to ignore irrelevant irritants, and when it is time to speak up before they reach their final straw.

Materials: Drawing paper (any paper works), drawing utensils (colored pencils, markers, or crayons)

1. Explain the saying, "The final straw," which means when a small irritant, when added to many small irritants, becomes unbearable. This often results in an angry reaction that appears out of proportion to the most recent annoyance.

2. Invite your client to create their own illustration to describe their experience of many small issues building up. Give examples like, "The final droplet that caused the spill," "The last marble that tipped the scales," or "The final juggling ball that made them fall." Or your client can stick with the original saying.

3. Ask your client to roughly draw their metaphor, illustrating generally how big the pile (of hay, droplets, marbles, balls, or other) has become in their own relationship.

4. Guide your client to imagine zooming in to look at details in their image. They may close their eyes if they would like. Ask how many irritants they imagine. Ask if the irritants are similar or different.

5. Invite your client to return to their paper to reveal more of their story by adding details, colors, or labels based on what they imagined.

6. Distinguish between "being able to handle a lot" and "wanting to handle a lot." Prompt your client to use lines or colors to show their preferred limit.

Discussion questions:

- Let's look at your image together. How much built up before it was too much? Tell me about your preferred limit.

- What did you notice when imagining looking closely at the details of your pile? What is it like to look at the whole, all piled up?

- If you were solving the problem of "The straw that broke the camel's back" (or use an alternative metaphor), what would you advise?

Helpful tip: Validate clients who value being able to handle a lot. This trait has likely served them well in many aspects of life. Explore times this characteristic is helpful, and then gently challenge them to consider times it is not. Help your client to try on new beliefs, like "I can handle a lot *and* I can choose when I don't want to."

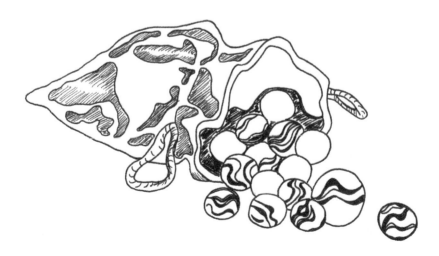

★ LINED-UP EXPECTATIONS

We all have expectations of each other, whether big or small, and whether we realize it or not. Those who believe they expect nothing of others may have been taught they are not allowed to have needs. Others may lower their expectations to avoid disappointment. In contrast, some may regularly have high expectations and never feel satisfied. Over time, unnamed needs, minimized hopes, or unrealistic expectations can lead to unfulfillment, resentment, and anger. This activity helps clients line up their expectations against skills, willingness, and time to help them realign their expectations for greater relationship satisfaction.

Materials: Drawing paper (any paper works), drawing utensils (colored pencils, markers, or crayons)

1. Instruct your client to draw five vertical lines on their paper and label them "expectation," "value," "skill," "willingness," and "time." Explain that each line is a scale—the bottom represents the least amount of expectation, value, skill, willingness, and time, and the top represents the most.

2. Instruct your client to identify a need or desire they have in their friendship, partnership, work, or family relationship.

3. Direct your client to place a dot on the expectation scale to indicate how high or low their expectation is for having that need met. Prompt them to place a dot on the value scale to indicate the value they place on this need.

4. Now ask your client to mark the remaining scales from low to high to match their counterpart's skill, willingness, and time to fulfill the need.

5. Invite your client to draw a line connecting each dot, from one scale to the next.

6. Repeat steps two through five with a different need or desire. Suggest your client use a new color for ease of distinguishing the lines.

Discussion questions:

- How do your expectations match up against your values? Do high-value needs have higher expectations, or not?

- How straight or jagged are the lines across all the scales? What does that say about the alignment or misalignment between your expectations and your counterpart's skill, willingness, and time?

- Which scales could most easily be adjusted to create more alignment? What would need to happen in real life to better align the scales?

Helpful tip: Use this activity with pairs. Ask one person to complete the "expectation" and "value" scale, and prompt the other person to complete the "skill," "willingness," and "time" scale. Or repurpose this activity to help individual clients match up the expectations they place on themselves with their values, skill, willingness, and time.

★ WALK AWAY WARMUP

Walking away can be difficult, whether it is from an argument or a chronically conflictual relationship. Angry individuals and those suffering because of others' anger stay in conflict for countless reasons, including feeling paralyzed or believing that walking away means the other person has won. Sometimes it is love, or a fear of losing love, that prevents someone walking away. This activity helps clients clarify what keeps them in conflict while warming up their imagination to picture what is needed for them to walk away.

Materials: Drawing paper (any paper works), drawing utensils (colored pencils, markers, or crayons), tape

1. Discuss how and when walking away from conflict may be a healthy choice. Tailor the discussion to your client's circumstances, being careful to assess for safety. For some, walking away might mean pausing a discussion until anger subsides, whereas others may be considering long-term plans to leave a hurtful relationship.

2. Ask your client to rip a piece of paper in half, lengthways, and tape the two pieces together to create one extra-long strip.

3. On the bottom of the strip of paper, prompt your client to illustrate their experience of conflict using colors, shapes, words, patterns, or symbols.

4. Now invite your client to imagine moving away from the conflict. Ask what internal or external barriers they encounter, such as emotions, beliefs, urges, or external blocks. Prompt them to add colors, shapes, words, patterns, or symbols to illustrate barriers.

5. Ask your client to imagine moving past the barriers. Invite them to illustrate being out of conflict by adding colors, shapes, words, patterns, or symbols further up their strip of paper. Let them know it's okay to feel relieved, anxious, angry, lonely, joyful, hurt, tired, or a combination of feelings.

6. Invite your client to continue moving up the strip of paper, illustrating changing feelings as they move even further away from conflict.

Discussion questions:

- Let's look at the entire strip of paper. What do you notice about the images as they move further away from conflict? What changes or stays the same?

- Point to where you end up spending the most time. In what ways does that help or not help you or your relationship?

- What might you add, remove, or change about this image to make it easier to remove yourself from unproductive conflict?

Helpful tip: Discuss whether it is safe and appropriate to initiate reconnection with someone after time apart. Invite your client to make additions to their image that show how they can use time away wisely to make reconnecting easier.

★ PSYCHIC SABOTAGE

Human brains like to be efficient, which means sometimes using mental shortcuts to quickly interpret situations and anticipate problems. But while jumping to conclusions or trying to read others' minds may save time, these assumptions are often inaccurate. Mistaken assumptions about others' intentions and feelings can spark anger to protect us from threats that don't actually exist. This activity helps clients examine relationship facts, distinguish them from assumptions, and replace crystal ball predictions with concrete evidence.

Materials: Drawing paper (any paper works), drawing utensils (colored pencils, markers, or crayons)

1. Explain the downside of mental shortcuts like jumping to conclusions and falsely mindreading. Discuss common mental shortcuts or negative assumptions your client tends to make.

2. Prompt your client to draw a medium-sized circle in the center of their paper to represent a crystal ball.

3. Ask your client to write "psychic thinking" inside the circle and "facts" outside the circle.

4. Invite your client to use colors and fonts that they consider playful and mystical to write their negative assumptions, mindreading thoughts, or future-telling predictions inside the crystal ball.

5. Ask your client to add lines, shapes, symbols, or colors inside the crystal ball to illustrate feelings and sensations that accompany these cognitive distortions.

6. Next, ask your client what observation prompted each thought. Invite your client to illustrate observable facts outside the crystal ball by adding words, lines, shapes, symbols, or colors. For example, "psychic thinking:" "They didn't care I was home;" "facts:" "I saw them watching TV when I walked in the door."

Discussion questions:

- Describe the words, lines, shapes, symbols, or colors inside and outside the crystal ball. Does anything surprise you or stand out?

- If anger existed somewhere in this image, where would it be? You can add that now.

- How might you check the facts in real life? How might observable facts help influence your thoughts, feelings, and actions?

Helpful tip: Teach clients to decrease the power of psychic thinking throughout the week by using these three steps: (1) Notice when you have a psychic thought. (2) Say to yourself, "I notice my mind is making the magical thought that…" (3) Visualize the psychic thought floating within a crystal ball. Try practicing these steps together.

Conclusion

I think of therapy like panning for gold. You scoop dirt, silt, and clouded water into your pan, and you swish. You swish the water around and around, separating the elements, hoping to find a nice nugget of gold. Rocks, sand, pebbles. The water becomes clearer, but no gold. You scoop again and swish. Rocks, sand, pebbles, but no gold. You scoop again. The process continues but is neither tiresome nor disappointing. It is present-focused, exciting, and even hopeful.

Then you see it. Something shiny. Your heart jumps. You swish and swish, perhaps a little quicker now, but still consciously and delicately, so as not to spill. It becomes clearer. It is not a nugget but a tiny gold flake, and it is beautiful. You carefully pinch it from the silt and delicately place it into a miniature glass vial. You hold it up to the light, examining it with awe and admiration. Then you scoop dirt, silt, and clouded water into your pan again, and you swish.

I hope this book has given you the inspiration and tools to continue scooping and swishing. I hope the activities helped you to separate rocks, sand, and pebbles, un-muddy water, and to capture many golden moments of growth and healing.

Thank you for your work.

References

Aarts, H., Ruys, K., Veling, H., Renes, R., *et al.* (2010) "The art of anger: Reward context turns avoidance responses to anger-related objects into approach." *Psychological Science* 21, 10, 1406–1410.

Abbott, K., Shanahan, M., and Neufeld, R. (2013) "Artistic tasks outperform nonartistic tasks for stress reduction." *Art Therapy* 30, 2, 71–78.

Azarnioshan, B., Naderi, H., Asghar Shojaee, A., and Asghariganji, A. (2019) "The mediating role of resilience in the relationship between perceived parenting styles and anger management." *International Journal of School Health* 6, 3, 1–6.

Baas, M., De Dreu, C., and Nijstad, B. (2011) "Creative production by angry people peaks early on, decreases over time, and is relatively unstructured." *The Journal of Experimental Social Psychology* 47, 6, 1107–1115.

Balban, M.Y., Neri, E., Kogon, M.M., Zeitzer, J.M., Spiegel, D., and Huberman, A.D. (2023) "Brief structured respiration practices enhance mood and reduce physiological arousal." *Cell Reports Medicine* 4, 1, 100895. https://doi.org/10.1016/j.xcrm.2022.100895

Bowen, D., Greene, J., and Kisida, B. (2014) "Learning to think critically: A visual art experiment." *Educational Researcher* 43, 1, 37–44.

Carver, C. and Harmon-Jones, E. (2009) "Anger is an approach-related affect: Evidence and implications." *Psychological Bulletin* 135, 2, 183–204.

Conwaya, P. and Hefferonb, K. (2019) *The Extraordinary in the Ordinary: Skychology – An Interpretative Phenomenological Analysis of Looking Up at the Sky.* London: Birkbeck University of London.

Dana, D. (2020) *Befriending Your Nervous System: Looking Through the Lens of Polyvagal Theory.* Louisville, CO: Sounds True.

Doyle, J., Campbell, M., and Gryshchuk, L. (2021) "Occupational stress and anger: Mediating effects of resiliency in first responders." *Journal of Police and Criminal Psychology* 36, 463–472.

Ekman, P. (1992) "Are there basic emotions?" *Psychological Review* 99, 550–553.

Ekman, P. and Cordaro, D. (2011) "What is meant by calling emotions basic." *Emotion Review* 3, 4, 364–370.

Fancourt, D. and Finn, S. (2019) *What Is the Evidence on the Role of the Arts in Improving Health and Well-Being? A Scoping Review.* Copenhagen: WHO Regional Office for Europe.

Fleming, A. (2022) "'Don't take it out on our staff!' How did Britain become so angry?" *The Guardian*, August 4. www.theguardian.com/society/2022/aug/04/britain-angry-abusive-behaviour-staff

Ford, B., Tamir, M., Brunyé, T., Shirer, W., Mahoney, C., and Taylor, H. (2010) "Keeping your eyes on the prize: Anger and visual attention to threats and rewards." *Psychological Science* 21, 8, 1098–1105.

Förster, K. and Kanske, P. (2021) "Exploiting the plasticity of compassion to improve psychotherapy." *Current Opinion in Behavioral Sciences* 39, 64–71.

Förster, K. and Kanske, P. (2022) "Upregulating positive affect through compassion: Psychological and physiological evidence." *The International Journal of Psychophysiology 176*, 100–107.

Gallup (2022) *Gallup Global Emotions*. Washington, DC: Gallup World Poll. www.gallup.com/analytics/349280/gallup-global-emotions-report.aspx

Garfinkel, S., Zorab, E., Navaratnam, N., Engels, M., *et al.* (2016) "Anger in brain and body: The neural and physiological perturbation of decision-making by emotion." *Social Cognitive and Affect Neuroscience 11*, 1, 150–158.

Ghati, N., Killa, A., Sharma, G., Karunakaran, B., *et al.* (2021) "A randomized trial of the immediate effect of *Bee-Humming Breathing* exercise on blood pressure and heart rate variability in patients with essential hypertension." *Explore 17*, 4, 312–319.

Halmburger, A., Baumert, A., and Schmitt, M. (2015) "Anger as driving factor of moral courage in comparison with guilt and global mood: A multimethod approach." *European Journal of Social Psychology 41*, 1, 39–51.

Hass-Cohen, N. and Clyde Findlay, J. (2019) "The art therapy relational neuroscience and memory reconsolidation four drawing protocol." *The Arts in Psychotherapy 63*, 51–59.

Hensley, S. (2019) "Poll: Americans say we're angrier than a generation ago." NPR, June 26. www.npr.org/sections/health-shots/2019/06/26/735757156/poll-americanssay-were-angrier-than-a-generation-ago

Hinchey, L. (2018) "Mindfulness-based art therapy: A review of the literature." *Inquiries Journal 10*, 5, 1.

Iani, L., Lauriola, M., Chiesa, A., and Cafaro, V. (2019) "Associations between mindfulness and emotion regulation: The key role of describing and nonreactivity." *Mindfulness 10*, 366–375.

Isis, P., Bokoch, R., Fowler, G., and Hass-Cohen, N. (2023) "Efficacy of a single session mindfulness-based art therapy doodle intervention." *Art Therapy*, April. https://doi.org/10.1080/07421656.2023.2192168

Kaimal, G., Kendra, R., and Muniz, J. (2016) "Reduction of cortisol levels and participants' responses following art making." *Art Therapy 33*, 2, 74–80.

Keltner, D. [Host] (2023) "Why we should look up at the sky" [Audio podcast episode]. *The Science of Happiness Podcast*. Greater Good, Berkeley, January 19.

Klussman, K., Curtin, N., Langer, J., and Nichols, A. (2020) "Examining the effect of mindfulness on well-being: Self-connection as a mediator." *Journal of Pacific Rim Psychology 14*. https://doi.org/10.1017/prp.2019.29

Lerner, J.S. and Keltner, D. (2001) "Fear, anger, and risk." *Journal of Personality and Social Psychology 81*, 1, 146–159.

Lerner, J.S. and Shonk, K. (2010) "How anger poisons decision making." *Harvard Business Review Magazine*, September. https://hbr.org/2010/09/how-anger-poisons-decision-making

Lieberman, M., Eisenberger, N., Crockett, M., Tom, S., Pfeifer, J., and Way, B. (2007) "Putting feelings into words." *Psychological Science, 18*, 5, 421–428.

Lindebaum, D. and Geddes, D. (2015) "The place and role of (moral) anger in organizational behavior studies." *Journal of Organizational Behavior 37*, 5, 738–757.

Long, K., Kim, E., Chen, Y., Wilson, M., Worthington Jr., E., and VanderWeele, T. (2020) "The role of hope in subsequent health and well-being for older adults: An outcome-wide longitudinal approach." *Global Epidemiology 2*, 100018.

Louie, D., Brook, K., and Frates, E. (2016) "The laughter prescription: A tool for lifestyle medicine." *American Journal of Lifestyle Medicine 10*, 4, 262–267.

Lusebrink, V. (2014) "Art therapy and the neural basis of imagery: Another possible view." *Journal of the American Art Therapy Association 30*, 2, 87–90.

Martin, L., Oepen, R., Bauer, K., Nottensteiner, A., *et al.* (2018) "Creative arts interventions for stress management and prevention-systematic review." *Behavioral Sciences 8*, 2, 28.

Nan, J., Hinz, L., and Lusebrink, V. (2021) "Clay Art Therapy on Emotion Regulation: Research, Theoretical Underpinnings, and Treatment Mechanisms." In C.R. Martin, L.-A. Hunter, V.B. Patel, V.R. Preedy, and R. Rajendram (eds) *The Neuroscience of Depression: Features, Diagnosis, and Treatment*. Cambridge, MA: Academic Press.

Nestor, J. (2020) *Breath: The New Science of a Lost Art*. London: Penguin Life.

Newland, O. and Bettencourt, A. (2020) "Effectiveness of mindfulness-based art therapy for symptoms of anxiety, depression, and fatigue: A systematic review and meta-analysis." *Complementary Therapies in Clinical Practice 41*, 101246. doi: 10.1016/j.ctcp.2020.101246

Porges, S.W. (2022) "Polyvagal theory: A science of safety." *Frontiers in Integrative Neuroscience 16*, 871227. www.frontiersin.org/articles/10.3389/fnint.2022.871227/full

Reddan, M., Wager, T., and Schiller, D. (2018) "Attenuating neural threat expression with imagination." *Neuron 100*, 4, 994–1005.

Roberts, R., Wiebels, K., Sumner, R., van Mulukom, V., *et al.* (2017) "An fMRI investigation of the relationship between future imagination and cognitive flexibility." *Neuropsychologia 95*, 156–172.

Schmitt, A., Gielnik, M., and Seibel, S. (2019) "When and how does anger during goal pursuit relate to goal achievement? The roles of persistence and action planning." *Motivation and Emotion 43*, 205–217.

Schornick, Z., Ellis, N., Ray, E., and Snyder, B. (2023) "Hope that benefits others: A systematic literature review of hope theory and prosocial outcomes." *International Journal of Applied Positive Psychology 8*, 37–61.

Segal-Engelchin, D., Huss, E., and Sarid, O. (2021) "The use of online CB-art interventions in the context of COVID-19: Enhancing salutogenic coping." *International Journal of Environmental Research and Public Health 18*, 4, 2057.

Segal-Engelchin, D., Achdut, N., Huss, E., and Sarid, O. (2020) "CB-art interventions implemented with mental health professionals working in a shared war reality: Transforming negative images and enhancing coping resources." *International Journal of Environmental Research and Public Health 17*, 7, 2287.

Sunseri, J. [Host] (2019) "Deb Dana: Story follows state, climbing the ladder and diagnosing" [audio/video podcast episode]. In The Polyvagal Podcast, August 27, https://youtu.be/tUzCnBec-2A?si=pH_Lw30H1zuu5TdV

Torre, J. and Lieberman, M. (2018) "Putting feelings into words: Affect labeling as implicit emotion regulation." *Emotion Review 10*, 2, 116–124.

Torres-Marín, J., Navarro-Carrillo, G., and Carretero-Dios, H. (2018) "Is the use of humor associated with anger management? The assessment of individual differences in humor styles in Spain." *Personality and Individual Differences 120*, 193–201.

Trivedi, G., Sharma, K., Saboo, B., Kathirvel, S., *et al.* (2023) "Humming (simple Bhramari Pranayama) as a stress buster: A Holter-based study to analyze heart rate variability (HRV) parameters during bhramari, physical activity, emotional stress, and sleep." *Cureus 15*, 4, e37527.

Tselebis, A., Bratis, D., Roubi, A., Anagnostopoulou, M., Giotakis, K., and Pachi, A. (2022) "Anger management during the COVID-19 lockdown: The role of resilience and family support." *Encephalos 59*, 1–10.

Veraksa, N., Gavrilova, M., and Veraksa, A. (2022) "'Complete the drawing!' The relationship between imagination and executive functions in children." *Education Sciences 12*, 2, 103.

Weiblen, R., Mairon, N., Krach, S., Buades-Rotger, M., *et al.* (2021) "The influence of anger on empathy and theory of mind." *PLOS One 16*, 7.

Williams, R. (2017) "Anger as a basic emotion and its role in personality building and pathological growth: The neuroscientific, developmental and clinical perspectives." *Frontiers in Psychology 8*, 1950.

World Economic Forum (2019) "Decline in human empathy creates global risks in the 'age of anger.'" Global risks, April 8. www.zurich.com/en/knowledge/topics/global-risks/decline-human-empathy-creates-global-risks-age-of-anger

Wu, R., Liu L., Zhu, H., Su, W., *et al.* (2019) "Brief mindfulness meditation improves emotion processing." *Frontiers in Neuroscience 13*, 1074. doi: 10.3389/fnins.2019.01074.

Further Reading and Resources

Other books by this author

Curtis, Erica (2022) *Art Therapy Activities for Kids: 75 Evidence-Based Art Projects to Improve Behavior, Build Social Skills, and Boost Emotional Resilience.* Oakland, CA: Rockridge Press.

Curtis, Erica and Ho, Ping (2019) *The Innovative Parent: Raising Connected, Happy, Successful Kids through Art.* Athens, OH: Ohio University Press/Swallow Press.

Online resources

Art therapy information and resources

American Art Therapy Association: www.arttherapy.org

British Association of Art Therapists: www.baat.org

International Expressive Arts Therapy Association®: www.ieata.org

Therapist locators

Art Therapy Credentials Board, Inc.: www.atcb.org/find-a-credentialed-art-therapist

Psychology Today: www.psychologytoday.com

Mental health helplines/crisis support

NAMI (National Alliance on Mental Illness): www.nami.org/help

SAMHSA (Substance Abuse and Mental Health Services Administration): www.samhsa.gov/find-help/national-helpline

Social emotional arts programming and events

Arts & Healing Initiative: www.artsandhealinginitiative.org

List of Activities